Rites of  Saxon and Norse Paganism:

Blót, Symbel, and Other Rites

Eric Wodening

Rites of Anglo-Saxon and Norse Paganism:
Blót, Symbel, and Other Rites

Eric Wodening

All Rights Reserved
©2003 Eric Wodening

First Edition Published 2003 by Café Press
Second Edition Published 2015 CreateSpace

ISBN-13: 978-1544077130
ISBN-10: 1544077130

Cover Illustration: "Offerscene" by J. Lund (circa 1827)

Table of Contents

Knowest How to Blót:
The Why and How of Heathen Sacrifice

Knowest how to pray
Knowest how to blót.
(*Hávamál* verse 144, line 3)

Foreword

Many, perhaps most religions involve some form of sacrifice. Indeed, sacrifice or blót, as it is more properly called in our faith, is central to the practice of heathendom. But while some form of sacrifice can be found in many religions, the reasons for performing sacrifices and how they are performed tend to vary.

Unfortunately the elder heathen left behind no handbooks on the subject. Modern heathen cannot simply go to the library and check out *How to Conduct a Proper Blót*, written by some elder heathen scholar. Fortunately, the elder heathen and their immediate descendants left behind a few sources which describe blót in some detail, some of which offers hints as to why blóts were offered to the gods. It is through examining these sources that one can learn not only how to perform blóts, but the reasons they are performed as well.

The Meaning of Blót

Both as a verb and as a noun the *blót* occurred in various Germanic languages. Gothic *blotan*, Old English *blótan*, and Old High German *blozan* all meant "to sacrifice", while Old Norse *blóta* meant "to worship" as well. As a noun *blót* occurred in both Old English and Old Norse. In Old English it simply meant "sacrifice", although in Old Norse *blót* also meant "worship" and "idol" as well. The words may have also occurred in Gothic. In his translation of the New Testament, Ulfilas rendered the Greek words *latreia*, "service to the gods; divine worship", and *sebasma* "an object of awe or worship" with the word *blutinassus*. This could well point to a Gothic cognate of *blót*.

The word *blót* appears to be related to Old English *blétsian*, modern English *bless*. In turn *blétsian* derives from the same root as modern English *blood* (a word found in most of the ancient Germanic languages). *Blétsian* may have originally meant "to mark as to hallow with blood". Perhaps the word *blót* originally meant "blood sacrifice" or "Hallowing with blood, blessing".

This would appear to be borne out by the elder sources. In *Hákonar Saga goða* (from *Heimskringla*), Snorri described how the blood of sacrificed animals was sprinkled about the temple and on the gathered folk. The flesh of the slaughtered animal was then cooked and served to everyone present. Later in *Heimskringla* Snorri described how the folk compelled King Hákon, nominally Christian, to eat horse liver at a sacrificial feast.

Discussing these passages, Turville-Petre notes, "The meaning of the sacrificial feast, as Snorri saw it, is fairly plain. When blood was sprinkled over altars and men and the toasts were drank, men were symbolically joined with gods of war and fertility, and with their dead ancestors, sharing their mystical powers. This is a form of communion."[1]

Indeed, it is safe to assume that by blessing the temple and the gathered folk with sacrificial blood, the priests were quite simply spreading the mægen (Turville-Petre's "mystical powers") to both the sanctuary and those gathered within it. Edgar Polomé once theorised that the purpose of the procession of Nerthus's wain (as described in Tacitus's *Germania*) was to spread the goddess's power (in heathen terms, *mægen*) about the countryside.[2] Blessing with sacrificial blood would then appear to share the same purpose as the procession of Nethurs's wain--to endow the community with divine mægen in order to ensure its continued success.

Blessing with sacrificial blood was not the only means by which divine mægen was spread during blót, as eating the flesh of the sacrificial animal would probably have the same effect. In fact, the sacrificial feast may have additional significance. In noting the association of Freyr (OE *Fréa*) with the boar, Turville-Petre expresses the suspicion that the boar was one of the forms Freyr took. He notes that the word *vaningi* "son of the Vanir" was applied to both Freyr and the boar in poetry and that a byname of Freyr's sister, Freyja, was *Sýr* "sow". According to Turville-Petre, "This implies that when the flesh of the boar was consumed at a sacrificial banquet, those who partook of it felt they consuming the god himself and absorbing his power."[3] This could be used as further evidence that the elder heathen saw the blót as a form of communion with the gods.

That the Germanic peoples may have regarded blót as a form of communion may be shown by the Gothic word *hunsl* and its Old English cognate *húsel*. In this Gothic translation of the New Testament, Ulfilas rendered the Greek Word *thusia* "sacrifice" and *latreia* "divine worship" with the word *hunsl*.

3

Old English *húsel* also meant "sacrifice" and was used as such in a translation of *Matthew* chapter 12, verse 7, but it was also used for "Eucharist" or "Christian Communion" *Húsel* survived into modern English as *housel*, a term used until relatively recently for "Eucharist". Oddly enough, while both Gothic *hunsl* and Old English *húsel* occur in decidedly non-Christian contexts, Old Norse *húsl* only occurs during the Roman Catholic era as a term for "Eucharist". It never appears in a heathen context. It is tempting to conclude that either Old Norse *húsl* was borrowed from Old English *húsel* (Anglo-Saxon missionaries were active in Scandinavia, after all) or that *húsl* never achieved importance among Old Norse speakers as a term for "sacrifice". Regardless, the use of Gothic *hunsl* and Old English *húsel* as terms for "sacrifice" and of the latter for "Eucharist" may imply that the elder heathen did indeed view blóts as a way of communing with the gods.

The elder sources reveal another purpose for blóts beyond communion. In *Víga-Glúms Saga* Þorkell the Tall wanted revenge on Glúm for driving him from his home, so he took an ox to Freyr's temple. He presented the animal to the god with the words, "Freyr, you who have long supported me and accepted many gifts and repaid them well, now I give you this ox so that Glúm may leave the land of Þverá…" In his account of the Rus, Arabic traveller Ibn Fadlan described how Rus traders would approach idols of the gods with gifts of silk, ale, meat, bread, and leeks in hope that the gods would help them get better prices for their goods.

In both of these cases it must be noted that individuals made sacrifices to the gods in the hope that the gods would grant their wishes in return. To the modern, non-heathen mind this might seem like nothing more than bribery, but Þorkell's words from *Víga-Glúms Saga* reveal that this was hardly the case. Þorkell stated that Freyr had "accepted many gifts from him" and "repaid them well." This reflects an ancient custom long held by the Germanic tribes that when one was given a gift, he was obliged to give a gift in return.[4] As the *Hávamál* states, "For a gift a similar gift should be given."

That the elder heathen saw blót as an exchange of earthly goods for divine blessings may also be seen in the Old English word *gield*, modern English *yield*. *Gield* meant "service, money, payment, tax, tribute, sacrifice". The verb *gieldan*, modern English *yield*, meant "to pay for, reward, requite", as well as "to worship, to sacrifice to". From these uses of *gield* and *gieldan* it may be surmised that the elder heathen viewed blót as a "down payment" to the gods for further blessings.

The elder heathen may have also seen blót in terms of wyrd, in which the past influences the present. At the centre of ancient Germanic cosmography stands the World Tree and the Well of Wyrd. Actions from the worlds within the Tree drop like dew into the Well, where they form the seething layers of the past. In turn these actions create an energy sources (not unlike water) which surges through the roots of the Tree to influence the present of the worlds contained within it.[5] As Bauschatz writes in *The Well and the Tree*, "The tree fills the well, the well nourishes the tree." [6]

Bauschatz viewed sacrifices made in bodies of water, such as the drowning of slaves to Nerthus described in Tacitus's *Germania*, as representative of the process of Wyrd. He observes that these actions "join the fertility celebrated in the ritual just performed with all favourable acts of fertility in the past…The ritual gets its power from the holy water of the well, to which all elements of ritual and the events finally return."[7] We might wish to go one step further than Bauschatz and suggest that all sacrifices, whether made into bodies of water or whether made with fertility or some other goal in mind, draw their power from the Well of Wyrd. That is, a blót is a means by which the folk seek to link results desired in the present (whether fertility, victory, or something else) with such favourable conditions as have occurred in the past. Indeed, it must be noted that when Þorkell sacrificed the ox to Freyr in *Víga-Glúms Saga*, he spoke of his relationship with Freyr and the gifts that they had exchanged in the past before addressing his concerns for revenge in the present. Quite simply, then, blóts are a way by which communities and individuals can improve their wyrds by invoking the past.

For the elder heathen blóts were a means of communion with the gods and receiving divine mægen in doing so. Blóts were also a way in which the folk could ensure gifts from the gods by giving gifts to the gods. Finally, blóts were a means by which communities could improve their wyrds by joining their hopes and desires for the present with such favourable results as had happened in the past.

What Was Sacrificed

In order to conduct a blót, the folk first needed something that they could give to the gods. As a result the Germanic tribes offered a variety of gifts to the Æsir and Vanir. And often the form of the blót was dictated by what was being sacrificed.

By far the most common sacrifices made to the gods were animals. The elder sources, from Roman reports of the Germanic peoples to the Icelandic sagas, often refer to the sacrifice of livestock. Evidence for the sacrifice of livestock is not only found in written sources, but through archaeology as well. At Yeavering in Northumberland, where an Anglo-Saxon heathen temple may have stood, a huge pile of ox bones was found.[8]

The sacrifice of a given animal in blót appears to have been determined by the god to whom the blót was being made. Swine were particularly sacred to Freyr and Freya (OE *Fréo*). *Heiðeks Saga* describes a boar blót to Freyr at length. References to sacrifices of boars can be found sprinkled throughout the elder sources, although the god to whom the swine was sacrificed is not always mentioned. A prose note to *Helgakviða Hjörvarþssonar* makes reference to the sacrificial boar.

Cattle also appear to have been holy to Freyr. Besides *Víga-Glúms Saga*, *Gísla Saga* also described the sacrifice of an ox to

Freyr. The *Brandkrossa Þattr* describes the sacrifice of a bull to Freyr. As Freyr is said to own Álfheimr, home of the elves, we should not be surprised when in *Kormáks Saga* a vovla tells an injured man to sacrifice a bull to the elves for healing.

Horses were closely associated with both Wóden (ON *Óðinn*) and Freyr. Perhaps for that reason it seems that often horse blóts were not to a specific god, but to all the gods. *Hákonar Saga goða* describes a horse sacrifice held at Hlaðir. *Flateyjarbók* describes how Olaf Tryggvasson arrived in Thrandheim to destroy a temple where horses were kept. There he found the folk in the middle of preparing a horse "for Freyr to eat."

Of course, the elder heathen sacrificed more than just livestock to the gods. As mentioned earlier, Ibn Fadlan told how Rus traders would bring gifts of silk, ale, meat, beer, and leeks to the gods. *The Life of Columbanus* mentions a large vessel of beer that the Alamanni meant to sacrifice to Wóden. It is conceivable that a portion of the ale drank at the sacrificial feasts mentioned in Icelandic sources and the ale drank at symbel was sacrificed to the gods.

Human sacrifice was extremely rare among the Germanic peoples, although it did sometimes occur. Unlike animal sacrifices, the victim was not eaten afterwards (the ancient Germanic peoples found cannibalism as revolting as we do today). Human sacrifices appear to have taken place only under very special circumstances.

War time was one of those circumstances when human sacrifice took place. Jordanes tells how the Goths sacrificed prisoners of war to "Mars". According to the Roman *Annals*, when the Hermenduri and the Chatti went to war with each other, the former promised to sacrifice men, horses, and weapons to "Mercury" and the latter promised to sacrifice the same to "Mars". Procopius told how the Germanic tribes would sacrifice the first prisoner of war to "Ares".

A particularly gruesome form of war time sacrifice performed by the Scandinavians was the "blood eagle (ON *blóðörn*)", in which the ribs were separated from the back and the lungs removed. According to the *Þáttr of Ragnars sonum*, Ragnar Loðbrók's sons avenged his death by carving the blood eagle upon his killer, King Ella of Northumbria. *Orneyinga Saga* describes how Torf-Einer, Jarl of Orkney, sacrificed Hálfdan Highleg to Óðinn by cutting the blood eagle into him. Not only does the blood eagle appear to have been a wartime sacrifice, but it also appears to have been reserved for one's worst enemies. In most cases it is performed by sons avenging their fathers' deaths.

Criminals also appear to have been sacrificed in a sacral version of the death penalty. In *Kristni Saga* when the Althing debated conversion to Christianity, the Christian faction complained heathen sacrificed the worst men, hurling them over cliffs and rocks. Both *Eyrbyggja Saga* and *Landnámabók* state that criminals were sentenced to be sacrificed. Under Frisian law anyone who stole a holy object from a temple was to have his ears slit, that he was to be castrated, and that he was to be staked out on the beach as a sacrifice to the gods.

Human sacrifices were also sometimes made when disasters struck. *Gautreks Saga* details how during a famine, the people of Gautland would voluntarily throw themselves off a cliff, believing they would go straight to Valhöll. *Ynglinga Saga* tells of a famine in Sweden during the reign of King Dómaldi. The first year oxen were sacrificed, but the crops still failed. The second year the Swedes resorted to human sacrifice, with no improvement in the harvest. The third year the Swedes decided that King Dómaldi's luck had failed him and sacrificed him to the gods.

A disaster other than famine resulted in what may be the most famous sacrifice of a king. Both Saxo Grammaticus and *Gautreks Saga* told how Starkaó was forced to sacrifice King Víkar. The king, Starkaó, and their crew had found themselves stranded off an island's coast. They cast lots to see how they might get a good wind and divined that one of them must be sacrificed to Óðinn. When they drew lots to see who should be sacrificed, it was King Víkar who was chosen. Not particularly wanting to sacrifice their king, the crew decided to hold a mock sacrifice. They made a noose of calf gut and hung it on a drooping, slender twig of a fir tree. The noose was then put around King Víkar's neck and Starkað poked him with a reed, saying, "Now I give thee to Óðinn." the reed then became a spear, the calf's gut became a strong rope, and the slender twig became a sturdy branch. King Víkar was raised aloft and hanged to death.

Although the sacrifice of kings was hardly common occurrence, Dómaldi and Víkar were not the only kings to be sacrificed to the gods. Among the Germanic peoples the king embodied the luck of the tribe. If the king had plenty of luck, there would be plenty of crops at harvest. If the king's luck failed, the crops would fail as well. When a king's luck failed, the folk deposed of him by sacrificing him to the gods.[9] When King Olaf Tretelglia as Sweden did not perform the proper blóts expected of a king, the crops failed. The Swedes then made King Olaf a sacrifice to Óðinn by burning him in his house.

As stated earlier, human sacrifice occurred very rarely among the Germanic peoples and only under special circumstances. Much more typical were the blóts of animals and other goods at the various festivals, through which the folk communed with the gods.

How Blóts Were Performed

All rituals follow some order. The blóts performed by the elder heathen were no different. We are fortunate that some of the elder sources actually describe blóts, sometimes in some detail. Perhaps the best source for the ritual's structure is the blót of animals that took place at Hlaðir as described in *Hákonar Saga goða*, from Snorri's *Heimskringla*.

According to Snorri, when a blót was to be held the folk would all come to the temple. They would bring with them everything they needed throughout the festival, including ale and livestock. The livestock, both cattle and horses, were slaughtered and the blood collected into vessels. The blood was then sprinkled over the altars and the temple walls and upon the gathered folk. The flesh of the slaughtered animals was boiled in kettles and served to everyone present. Goblets were filled with ale and the ale was blessed by the host in charge of the blót. Toasts were then made to Óðinn, for victory and power to the king, and Njörðr and Freyr for frith and good harvest. The host then drank the bragarfull, following which the folk drank toasts in memory of those who had died.

Looking at Snorri's account we can break the blót down into its various stages. Supplementing it with information from other sources we can then develop a fairly good picture of what was involved in blóting livestock.

I. Slaughter: As stated earlier, livestock were by far the most common gifts to be given to the gods. Many, if not most, ancient blóts probably involved the slaughter of animals. Unfortunately, the elder sources do not document the procedure for the slaughter of livestock for blót in any great detail.

Regardless, through careful examination of the elder sources we can glean some details of the ritual involved in the sacrificial slaughter of animals. Some of that ritual apparently took place before the animals was even slain. *Heiðreks Saga* describes how the sacrificial boar or *sonargöltr* ("the leading boar") was led before the king at Yuletide. So holy was the boar regarded that the folk would place their hands upon him to swear oaths. *Helgasviða Hjörvarþssonar* also tells how on Yule Eve the sacrificial boar was led into the hall and men swore oaths upon him while drinking the bragarfull. It is impossible to know whether the custom of swearing oaths on the sacrificial board was confined to Yuletide or performed at other holy tides as well. It is also impossible to know whether the folk swore oaths upon other sacrificial animals or the custom was confined to boars. At any rate both *Heiðreks Saga* and *Helgasviða Hjörvarþssonar* demonstrate that some ritual took place even before the animal was slaughtered for blót.

Both of these sources also demonstrate that sacrificial animals were treated with a great deal of reverence, something confirmed to a degree by other sources *Hrafnkes Saga* told how Hrafnkell Freysgoði kept a stallion dedicated to Freyr and that Hrafnkell had sworn no one would ride the horse against his will, under penalty of death. When Hrafnkell's shepherd rode the horse, he felt obliged to kill the shepherd. According to *Flateyjarbók* the temple at Thrandheim kept a herd of horses specifically dedicated to the god. When Olaf Tryggvason desecrated the temple, he rode the stallion of the herd. Although not stated outright, it seems clear that Olaf did this as an insult to Freyr. These instances make it clear that animals dedicated to the gods, which would include sacrificial animals, were given special treatment (i.e. sacred horses were not ridden, etc.) and regarded with a high degree of reverence. It is safe to assume that any intentional cruelty to these animals would have been considered blasphemy.

According to the elder sources, the ancient Germanic peoples used a variety of methods to slay sacrificial animals. In his description of the great temple at Uppsala, Adam of Bremen described how at a festival was held every nine years, nine of every male animal was hanged to the gods. Ibn Rustah, an Arab who wrote about the Norsemen in 10th Century Russia, told how they hanged victims on a pole as sacrifices to the gods. Hanging was perhaps closely associated with Wóden. Verses 138 to 139 of the *Hávamál* tell how Óðinn hanged from the World Tree, wounded by a spear, as a sacrifice to himself, winning the runes as a result. As discussed earlier, both Saxo and *Gautreks Saga* describe how King Víkar was hanged as a sacrifice to Óðinn.

Sacrificial victims were also drowned. In *Germania* Tacitus related how slaves who served the goddess Nerthus were drowned in lakes as sacrifices to her. A marginal note attached to Adam of Bremen's description of the temple at Uppsala mentions a well where sacrifices were performed. According to Orosius, the Cimbri drowned horses in a river as sacrifices to the gods following a victory over the Romans. Drowning could have been a method of sacrifice particularly associated with the Vanir.[10] Indeed, in *Ynglinga Saga*, Freyr's son Fjölnir drowned in a mead vat.

Of course, to the modern mind the most obvious means of slaying an animal may be slashing his throat or beheading him. Unfortunately the elder sources make few references to sacrifices being slain in such a way. In his description of a Norse chieftain's funeral, Ibn Fadlan described how a hen was beheaded and then tossed into the funeral ship. The precise significance of this act is beyond the scope of this article, but part of the reason the hen was beheaded may have been as a blót either to the gods or the dead chieftain. Although rarely mentioned in the elder sources, the very simplicity of slashing an animal's throat or beheading it makes it at least possible that some blót animals were slain in such as way.

From all appearances some ritualistic formula accompanied the slaying of a blót animal. In *Víga-Glúms Saga*, when Þorkell sacrificed an ox to Freyr, he offered a prayer that included the words, "I give you this ox…" In both *Gautreks Saga* and Saxo's account, Starkað sacrificed King Víkar with the words, "Now I give you to Óðinn." It seems likely that a ritual formula was uttered upon slaying a sacrificial victim, almost always some variant on the words "I give (whatever the particular victim may be) to (whomever the particular god to whom the blót was being made)." Oftentimes this formula was probably accompanied by a prayer stating some request, as in the case of Þorkell in *Víga-Glúms Saga*. Þorkell not only told Freyr that he was giving the ox to the god, but he also asked Freyr to drive Glúm from Þverá in return.

II. Blessing: As stated earlier, the word *blót* may be related to the Old English world *blétsian*, modern English *bless*, which

12

may have originally meant "to mark as to hallow with blood". According to Snorri such hallowing with blood or blessing took place once the animals had been slaughtered.

Snorri explained in *Hákonar Saga goða* that the blood from the sacrificial animals was called *hlaut* and that it was drained into vessels called *hlautbollar*. The sacrificial blood or *hlaut* was then sprinkled over the altars, the temple walls, and the gathered folk with *halutteinar*. What Snorri described was obviously the "hallowing with blood" for which Old English *blétsian* was originally applied.

The term *hlaut*, which Snorri stated the blood was called, appears to be related to the Old Norse word *hlútr* (a variant spelling of which was *hlautr*). According to Cleasby and Vigfusson's *Icelandic-English Dictionary*, *hlaut* may have been an abbreviated form of the hypothetical word *hlautblóðr*--that is, sacrificial blood that was used to mark lots used in divination. Indeed, the word *hlauttein* was not only applied to the branches used to bless the temple and the folk, but to lots used in divination (apparently blessed by sacrificial blood) as well. Other terms for lots used in divination, *hlautvíðr* and *blótspan*, also reflect the practice of blessing lots with sacrificial blood. The purpose of marking lots with sacrificial blood was probably the same as sprinkling the blood upon the temple and the folk--to bless them and endow them with the divine mægen.

References to the "hallowing with blood" or blessing appear in sources other than *Hákonar Saga goða*. *Eyrbygja Saga* describes how the sacrificial blood (called *hlaut* here as well) should be sprinkled from the hlautbolli In *Hyndluljóð* Freyja boasted how her follower Óttar reddened an altar with blood so that it turned to glass. In *Kormáks Saga* a wise woman advised a wounded man who wished to be healed to sacrifice a bull to the elves and to redden the elf mound with its blood. From these various sources it would appear that the hallowing with blood or blessing was central to blót.

13

III. Boiling the Meat: While the blood of the sacrificial animal was used to bless the temple and the gathered folk, according to Snorri in *Hákonar Saga goða* the animal's flesh was boiled as meat for everyone present. In the temple the fire occupied the middle of the floor and over it hung the kettles in which the meat was boiled. Making a feast of the sacrificial animal's flesh was apparently a very old custom among the Germanic peoples. A Gothic word for "sacrifice", *sauþs*, is cognate to Old Norse *sjóða* and Old English *séoþan* (Modern English *seethe*), both meaning "to cook, to boil". Gothic *sauþs* is then literally "That which is cooked" or "the sacrificial meat". Of course, the term could not have developed the meaning of "sacrifice" unless the sacrificial animals were butchered, cooked, and then served to the gathered folk at blót.

IV. Hallowing the Ale: In *Hákonar Saga goða* Snorri states that the blót ale was borne over the fire and then the sign of the hammer was made over it. It is difficult to ascertain the significance of the ale being borne over the fire. On the one hand it seems possible that passing the ale over the fire was a means of consecrating it. In some ways this would resemble the rite of need fire. The need fire could only be lit by a fire bow or a fire drill, it could not be lit by flint and steel. Once lit, livestock were driven through the fire in the hope that it would drive away pests and disease. The power of fire to stave off disease and drive away evil spirits was also reflected in the custom of nobility often sleeping with candles in their rooms. Passing the ale over the fire could then be a means of sanctifying the ale, of driving any evil influences away from it. On the other hand, bearing the ale over the fire could simply have been a means of getting it from one side of the hall to another. After all, if the fire is located in the middle of the hall, the ale vat on one side of the hall, and the host in charge of the blót on the other side, then it would have to be passed over the fire at some point.

We are on firmer ground with regards to making the sign of the hammer over the ale. The practice of hallowing something by making the sign of the hammer over it appears to have been a very ancient custom in Scandinavia. In *Sigdrífumál* Sigdrífa advised Sigurðr to make the sign of the hammer over his cup. Later in *Hákonar Saga goða* when the Christian king Hákon made the sign of the cross over his cup during blót, many of the gathered heathen objected. One of the king's friends defended him by saying that the king had made the sign of the hammer over it before he drank. References to the hallowing with the sign of the hammer are found in *Egils Saga, Olafs Saga Helga, Flateyjarbók*, and many other sources. Considering the number of sources in which it appears and the possible antiquity of some of those sources (like most of the heroic lays of the *Poetic Edda, Sigdrífumál* may be one of the oldest poems in Old Norse literature), there is little reason to believe that making the sign of the hammer was borrowed from the Christian custom of making the sign of the cross.

The significance of making the hammer sign is easy to understand. The hammer is the weapon of Þunor (ON *Þórr*). As the primary defender of the gods and men from the forces of evil, Þunor appears to have been intimately linked to the act of consecration. Several memorial stones throughout Scandinavia, dating from the 10th and 11th centuries, bear the words *Þur viki...*, "May Þórr hallow..." Sometimes a picture of a hammer is also carved into the stone.[11] By making the sign of the hammer over the ale, then, it would be hallowed in the name of Þórr.

It seems apparent that some of the ale was poured out as a sacrifice to the gods. We know from both Ibn Fadlan's account and *The Life of St. Columbanus* that ale and beer were given as gifts to the gods by the ancient Germanic peoples. That some of the blót ale used to make the toasts in blót was shared with the gods may borne out by a statement in *Fagrskinna*, in which it is said that in older times the folk poured out the full as they now did the minni. This indicates that the full and minni (both terms for toasts that will be explained below) may have been poured out as a libation to the gods.

VI. The Full: According to Snorri, once the ale had been hallowed there followed a series of "toasts" or "full". The first was made to Óðinn (OE *Wóden*) for victory and might for the king. The second was made to Njörðr and Freyr (OE *Fréa*) for frith and a good harvest. Finally the folk drank toasts to dead kinsmen; according to Snorri such toasts were called *minni*.

These toasts such as Snorri described as taking place at Hlaðir are well attested in other sources. *Fagrskinna* confirms that toasts were made to Þórr and other gods. They also played a role in funerals, as in *Heimskringla* Sveinn Tjúguskegg drank a minni to his father. That same chapter the Jómsborg Vikings are said to drink toasts to Jesus and the archangel Michael. Of course, such toasts played a central role in the ritual of symbel.[12]

In *Hákonar Saga goða* Snorri does not say whether the full were drunk before or after the feast of the sacrificial meat. In *Germania* section 22 Tacitus specified that the Germanic people ate a meal before engaging in the drinking bouts he described in some detail. If this custom of eating before long drinking bouts survived into the Dark Ages, then it might be safe to assume the full were drunk after the feast was served. If this was the case, then the drinking of the full might constitute a ritual all its own, that of symbel.

The Old Norse word *full* simply meant a "drinking vessel" and came to be used for the toasts made at blót and symbel. It is cognate to the Old English word *ful*, also meaning "drinking vessel" (as in *medoful*, "mead cup"). The word *bragarfull* (also spelled *bragafull*) is a compound of *bragr*, meaning "the best, the foremost", and *full* "drinking vessel, toast". It appears to mean "the cup of the foremost" or "the leader's cup". Regardless, the *bragarfull* was a toast drank to the dead king or another deceased noble. It appears most frequently in the elder sources in descriptions of funerals, although it also appeared in other contexts as well (such as the blót described in *Hákonar Saga goða*). In *Ynglinga Saga* Snorri described how upon the death of a king or jarl, his heir would have to sit on the step in front of the high seat until he drank the bragarfull. Once he had done so he could take his place in the high seat as the new king or jarl.

The word *minni* which Snorri uses of toasts in memory of the dead had as its primary senses "memory", "memorials", and "memory of past times". It is not the only word used of the memorial toast, as there is also *minnishorn. minnisöl*, and *minnisveig*; however. Turville-Petre theorises that the use of *minni* for "toast of memory" must have been influenced by Old High German *minna*, which was used for little more than "toast".[13] In many cases *minni* appears to have been used as a synonym for *full* and was sometimes applied to the full drank to the gods. It is possible that *full* was the older of the two terms and that *minni* gradually took the place of *full*. This may be confirmed by *Fagrskinna*, in which it is said that "in the old days, people poured out the full as they now did the minni, and they assigned the full to their mightiest kinsmen, or else to Þórr and other gods."[14] Either *minni* came to mean "toast" under the influence of Old High German *minna* or it was originally applied to the memorial cup and later came to mean any full.

Conclusion

An animal blót appears to have taken place in various stages. First, there may have been some ritual before the slaughter of the animal such as leading the sacrificial boar before the king. Second, there was the slaughter of the animal itself. Third, there was the blessing, in which the animal's blood was sprinkled about the temple and upon the folk. Fourth, the blót ale was hallowed and may have been given as a libation to the gods. Finally, there were the full, made either at the beginning of the blót feast or in a symbel held afterwards.

Alongside symbel, blót is among the most important rituals in which a heathen can participate. It is a means by which heathen can commune with the gods. It is a means by which we can give gifts to the gods and thereby receive gifts from the gods in return. And it is a means by which heathen can improve their

17

wyrds by invoking such favourable conditions as had occurred in the past.

Wordhoard

bragarfull: also spelled *bragafull*. The toast to the dead king or chieftain.

full: An Old Norse word used for a drinking vessel or a toast. The plural is also *full*.

mægen: An Old English word meaning the spiritual or metaphysical energy permeating the worlds and possessed by all things, similar to the Polynesian concept of *mana*.

minni: An Old Norse word used for the toasts to the dead ancestors. Also used of any full.

symbel: (ON *sumbl*): The ritual drinking feast at which the participants try to place themselves into the flow of Wyrd through the binding of words and deeds .[15]

Bookhoard

Bauschatz, Paul. *The Well and the Tree*. Amherst, MA: University of Massachusetts Press, 1982.

Cleasby, Richard. Vigfusson, Gudbrand (eds.). *An Icelandic-English Dictonary*. Oxford: Clarendon Press, 1975.

Davidson, H. R. Ellis. *The Lost Beliefs of Northern Europe*. London: Routledge, 1993.

Davdison, H. R. Ellis. *Gods and Myths of Northern Europe*. Harmondsworth, England: Penguin books, 1964.

A Gothic Etymological Dictionary. Leiden, Neitehrlands: E.J. Bril.

Hall, Clark. (ed.) *A Concise Anglo-Saxon Dictionary.* Downsview, Canada. Universtiy of Toronto Press.

Leach Maria (ed.) *Funk and Wagnalls Standard Dictionary of Folklore, Mythology, and Legend.* New York: Harper and Row, 1972.

The Oxford New English Dictionary. New York: Oxford University Press.

Polomé, Edgar. "Indo-European Component in Germanic Religion." Jann Puuhvel (ed.). *Myth and Law among the Indo-Europeans.* Berkley: University of California Press, 1970.

Turville-Petere, E.O.G. *Myth and Religion of the North.* New York: Holt, Rineheart, and Winston, 1964.

Wodening, Eric. "An Anglo-Saxon Symbel." *Theod,* Watertown NY, Wælburges 1995.

Wodening, Eric. *Gods of the World: the Vanir in Ancient Heathenry.* Watertown, NY: Theod, 1996.

Wodening, Eric. *We Are Our Deeds.* Watertown, NY: Theod, 1998.

Endnotes

1 Turville-Petre. *Myth and Reilgion of the North,* p. 251 (hereafter Turville-Petre).

2 Wodening. *Gods of the World,* pp. 38-39.

3 Turville-Petre, p. 225.

4 Wodening. *We Are Our Deeds,* p. 67.

19

5. Bauuschatz, Paul. *The Well and the Tree*, pp. 1-24 (hereafter Bauchatz).

6 Baruchtaz, p. 64.

7 ibid.

8 Ellis-Davidson. *Lost Beliefs of Northern Europe*, p. 22.

9 Wodening. *Gods of the World*, pp. 21-29.

10. Wodening. *Gods of the World*, p. 36.

11. Turvile-PEtere. pp. 81-85.

12 See Wodening, Eric. "An Anglo-Saxon Symbel". pp. 11-20. *Theod*, Wælburges 1995.

13. Turville-Petre. p. 257.

14 ibid.

15 Bauschatz, pp. 109-110.

An Anglo-Saxon Symbel

Original version 1st published in Theod, volume II, issue 2,
Wælburges 1995

The Significance of Symbel

Perhaps no other rite in heathendom stands out as importantly
or as uniquely as symbel (OE *symbel*; OIcel *sumbl*). According
to Bauschatz, symbel is the ritual drinking feast at which the
participants try to place themselves into the flow of Wyrd
through the binding of words and deeds.[1] In other words, it is a
means by which the deeds of now are linked to those of the
past.

Quite a few elder sources refer to symbel. The phrase *sittien at
sumble* appears in the Old Saxon poem *Heliand*[2] and
essentially the same phrase appears in the Old English *DReam
of the Rood* (*sittan to symle*) and the Old Icelandic poem
Locasenna. The word "symbel" also appears in its various
forms in such diverse sources as *Hymiskviða, Judith*, and, of
course, *Beowulf*.[3] It appears to have been common to most of
the Germanic languages.

The origins of the word "symbel" are unknown. One of the
earliest etymologies theorised it was a borrowing of Latin
symbola, itself a borrowing of Greek *sumbole* "collection for a
meal". This etymology has never been widely accepted due to
phonological considerations and the fact that *symbel* appears
far too often in the purely Germanic sense of the ritual drinking
rite to be a borrowed word.[4] Bauschatz proposed that "symbel"
may derive from proto-Germanic *sum-* or *sam-* "gathering
together" and **alu* "ale". Using this etymology "symbel would

literally mean "a gathering of ale". [ibid] As the etymology implies, symbel appears to have been a group activity. There are no references to anyone having symbel alone.[5]

Solemnity seems to have been an earmark of symbel as well. The Old English word *symbelness* means not only "festivity", but "solemnity". This solemnity is not the dourness associated with some Christian church services, but rather "a sense of deep significance and importance".[6] In *Beowulf*, at Hróðgar's first symbel, "there was men's laughter, noise resounded/the words were winsome".[ibid] At symbel, frith and goodwill prevail (*Beowulf* lines 1016-1019). Symbelness, then, is a ritual mindset of determination to accomplish the ritual at hand.

Order also seems to have played a part in symbel. To "sit at symbel" implies order, in that sitting requires a place to sit and hence some organised distribution of seats.[7] In *Beowulf* we get only the vaguest hint of such an order. At the second symbel, Hróðgar sits with his nephew Hróðwulf; his þyle (spokesman) Unferð, sits at the king's feet (*Beowulf* 5, line 1165). Later Beowulf is described as sitting between Hróðgar's sons (*Beowulf* line 1190). The grouping of the greatest men together implies that some sort of order was used in determining the seating arrangements. The apportioning of seats was probably quite important at symbel, as such apportioning would represent such as done by Wyrd.[8]

As stated earlier, symbel was a ritual drinking feast. The preferred symbel drink was some sort of alcohol. In *Beowulf* the men are gathered in the *béorsele*, "beer hall" and it is an eolowæge, "ale cup", that is passed around.[9] The drink is never named in the symbel scenes of *Beowulf*, though it is in *Locasenna*: "And I blend the mead for them with evil."[10]

Whether the drink was mead or another alcoholic drink, the use of an intoxicant seems significant. Alcohol would allow for the altered mood needed to take the celebrants out of this space and time. More important is drinking's close relationship to the actions of the Well of Wyrd. Like the Well, the cup holds a liquid quite different from other liquids. The drinking at symbel is also accompanied by speech, just as the watering of the World Tree accompanies the Norns' decrees. The whole point of the drinking, indeed of symbel, is to bring the participants, their deeds, and their words into the flow of Wyrd. Symbel is in many ways, a re-enactment of the Norns, continuously speaking the orlæg while watering Yggdrasil.[11]

Symbel appears to have been held almost exclusively indoors. In *Beowulf* both symbels are held in Heorot, Hróðgar's hall, while in *Locasenna* the gods hold symbel in Ægir's hall. In no other sources is it made clear that a symbel was held outside.[12] Further the symbel hall (or perhaps we should say "symbelhouse" after Old English *symbelhús*) appears to have been decorated as befits a festival. In *Beowulf* Hróðgar ordered Heorot cleaned and decorated with finery (*Beowulf* lines 991-992). The celebration of symbel inside was probably meant to further remove the participants from the earthly time stream and place them into the timeless continuity of Wyrd, the symbelhouse acting as a barrier to the rest of the world. Decorations, such as those in *Beowulf*, may well have aided in this process.

The Order of Symbel

Symbel also seems, like all rites, to have had a specific order. The most detailed portrayal of symbel is in the two symbel scenes in *Beowulf*, where such an order is implied.

The second symbel scene in *Beowulf* begins with toasts exchanged between Hróðgar and Hróðwulf (*Beowulf* line 1015). While toasting to others' health was no doubt as common in the heathen era as it is today (probably more so), it seems possible that more than ordinary "toasts" were involved. A custom common to the Germanic peoples appears to have been that of the myne drink (Old Norse *minnisöl*) or "memory drink". The myne drink was drunk to one's ancestors as well as the gods. *Fagrskinna* states that myne drinks were made to Þorr and the other gods.[12] Indeed, myne drinking may appear in the context of symbel in *Heimskringla*. Svein call an erfiöl or "funeral feast" after the death of his father Harald (a rite very similar, if not identical to, symbel). At the beginning of this feast Svein drinks his father's myne, then takes the high seat and vows to attack Æþelræd in England within three years. Other mynes are made to Jesus and the archangel Michael following this. The myne drink also occurred in England and Germany and survived as the toasts to the dead at wakes and funeral feasts. It seems likely that Hróðgar and Hróðwulf may have made myne drinks to the gods and their forebears as well as exchanging toasts between themselves.

Following the "toasts" in the second symbel scene comes an exchange of gifts. Hróðgar gave Beowulf a banner, a helm, a coat of male, and a sword (*Beowulf* line 1020). Gift giving in the context of symbel seems to have a triple importance. First, there is a doctrine of giving common to all the Germanic peoples in which every gift demands a gift in return. To fail to do so would result in a loss of mægen ("magical power" or "luck") equal in worth to the gift.[13] Second, the giving of gifts associated with Beowulf's victory further binds the past and the present. The sword, in particular, as an ancient weapon forged by ettins, acts to merge past and present, given as it is to the hero of the day--Beowulf.[14] Finally, a dealing out of gifts could reflect the dealing done by Wyrd, much as the seating arrangement does.

Following the gift giving done at the second symbel, the scop "sings" of Finn's conflict with the Danes (*Beowulf* lines 1066-1159). A poem in a ritual or social context, such as symbel, was called in Old English a *léod*. The purpose of the *scopléod* (a léod "sang" by a scop) seems fairly obvious: through reciting an event from history the scop invokes the contents of the Well of the Wyrd, further strengthening the link between past and present

Another type of speech follows the scopléoð, these made by the symbel's celebrants: the *gielp* and *béot*. On the surfaces, gielps and béots appear to be the same, and the words are used almost interchangeably; however, there seem to have been some differences between the two. The gielp appears to have emphasised the glory that one's forebears or oneself have achieved in the past--what many would considered "bragging". The béot, on the other hand, emphasises the promise of an action, "plighting one's troth" literally.[15] Svein's vow to attack Æþelræd would constitute a béot.

The gielp and béot together compromised most of the speeches made at symbel. In the first symbel scene in *Beowulf*, Beowulf begins his speech with a gielp. He boasts of his kinship to Higelac and of his achievements in the pasat. From his gielp, Beowulf proceeds to his béot to slay Grendel, and ends it with the phrase "Gæð a wyrd swa hiio scel (*Beowulf*, line 455)," "Goeth ever Wyrd as she shall," thus bringing past deeds together with deeds coming to be. [16]

Following Beowulf's béot to slay Grendel and Hróðgar's acceptance of it, comes Unferð's challenge of Beowulf's abilities. Like Beowulf's gielp, it too is rooted in the past (through admittedly from Unferð's point of view). Specifically, Unferð's challenge refers to Beowulf's swimming match with Brecca, a match which fared badly for Beowulf, at least according to Unferð. (*Beowulf*, lines 499-529) The purpose of Unferð's challenge seems to have ben to test the overall validity of Beowulf's béot. If Beowulf's victories were truly through chance, and his true character was reflected in the swimming match as recounted by Unferð, then his béot to slay Grendel would be invalid.

Unferð's challenge could well be connected to his office of þyle. *Þyle* is glossed as "orator" in Old English sources, though there appears to be much more to it than that. In the *Hávamál* Wóden is referred to as *Fimbulþul*, "the Great Þyle", and prior to his advice to the man Loddfafnir he states that it is time to sit upon the þyle's stool and chant as a þyle. Similarly, figures such as Sigurðr's master Reginn are often referred to as þyles. This implies that the þyle dealt with the transmission of lore to others, to some degree or another.

The association of the þyle with the transmission of knowledge is strengthened by the Old Norse word *þula*, which means "a list of facts in poetic form" or "a poem that lists various facts in some sort of order". The two words appear somehow connected, so that a þyle would be someone who knows and recites þular.

Unferð's challenge may then well have a purpose. As a keeper of lore it may be the duty of the þyle to challenge béots that he suspects may not be kept.

Beowulf responds to Unferð's challenge with a gielp that we must assume is a more accurate account of the swimming contest. The gielp then proceeds to a challenge of Unferð's own character (he is said to have killed his own kin), then to a repeating of Beowulf's béot to slay Grendel (*Beowulf*, lines 530-606). Beowulf's response seems designed to reaffirm the validity of his béot by once more linking it to a deed he performed in the past (that it also denigrates the character of Unferð must be regarded as an added bonus).

Though *Beowulf* does not state this, it may be assumed that once each participant has made a gielp or a béot, the process begins again with the scop singing a léoð.

Within symbel there appear to have been four roles (besides the general role of "symbeler") necessary to the rite. The first of these can be called the *symbelgifa* (an Old English word meaning "one who gives or hosts a symbel). In *Beowulf* the role of symbelgifa fell to Hróðgar as lord of Heorot. Hróðgar played much more than the role of a simple host. As symbelgifa he seems to have been charged with arbitrating béots and challenges. After Beowulf's béot to slay Grendel, Hróðgar makes a speech (in the form of a gielp) accepting Beowulf's béot. Later, after Unferð's challenge to the béot, Hróðgar's acceptance is not made explicit, though his faith that Beowulf can slay Grendel implies it. That the symbelgifa would be charged with arbitrating béots and challenges would make sense. Left unchecked, a series of béots and challenges could easily degenerate into a shouting match between þyle and symbeler or, worse yet, violence. An absolute authority, such as the symbelgifa, who could weigh the validity of béots and challenges, would make such disruption less likely. In other ways the symbelgifa probably acted as a "master of ceremonies". He probably led the myne drinking and in part helped placed the participants in a state of "symbelness".

Another important role is that of the scop (pronounced "shawp"). In Anglo-Saxon England the scop was an official poet, attached to a noble household (the scop in *Beowulf* is called the *cyninges þegn*, "the king's thane"), and charged with reciting eulogies in praise of the king and his forebears. By

27

attracting the "sympathetic ear" of past rulers, the scop insured the well-being of the present king, the bearer of the national luck, and in doing so insured the well-being of the folk as well. Naturally to do his job, the scop had to be both a sound chronicler and historian.[17] The scop's position as an official reciter of praise can be seen in the use of the phrase *guman gilphlæden* "geilp laden man" to describe Hróðgar's scop.[18]

Though never stated, the scop may have acted as the recorder of deeds performed by present day heroes as well as the béots made at symbel; hence the scop may have aided the symbelgifa in arbitrating béots and challenges. That is, when consulted by the symbelgifa, the scop could confirm or deny any of the statements made. While never made explicit, this seems to be a logical extension of the scop's duties as chronicler and historian.

The third position necessary to symbel would be someone to serve the mead or beer, here called for convenience's sake, "the alekeeper". While reference is made to "thegns" serving the drink in *Beowulf*, this role seems to have fallen primarily to Wéalhþéow, Hróðgar's queen. At the first symbel, Wéalhþéow greets the warriors, then serves Hróðgar before going from warrior to warrior with the cup (*Beowulf*, lines 612-1614). In the second symbel the poem shows her serving only Hróðgar and Beowulf, though this does not rule out her serving others as well (*Beowulf*, lines 1167-1232). While in charge of the overall serving arrangements, the alekeeper would have her assistants to help serve the drink, as the reference to "serving thegns" indicates such.

The serving of the cup to each symbeler seems to have been accompanied by words of praise of the one being served. Again, this is probably to merge words with the flow of Wyrd; if pleasant words are said of someone, then perhaps he shall have a pleasant wyrd as well. Bauschatz observes that the "presence of a noblewoman (Wéalhþéow) at the drinking of the intoxicant adds the additional elements of the female nurture."[19] though Wéalhþéow's presence may have a deeper meaning than that. If it is taken that the ale is symbolic of the water of the Well of the Wyrd and its pouring symbolic of the Norns watering Yggsdrasill, then it follows that the alekeeper (in *Beowulf*, Wéalhþéow) would symbolise Wyrd herself. Hence, the symbel ritual is in many ways a re-enactment of the entire process of Wyrd itself.

The fourth role in symbel would be that of the þyle. The þyle would be charged with challenging any béots that he feels might not be kept by the individual making them. In many ways the þyle would act as a prosecuting attorney, with the symbelgifa as the judge.

It must be noted that in *Beowulf* that neither the scop nor the alekeeper are portrayed as drinking. While this is not specified in any of the sources, the two, as the only possible non-drinking participants, may have seen the symbel did not get out of hand. It makes sense that they would have the power, should anyone get too drunk or, worse yet, sick, to end the rite. It must be stressed again that this is <u>not</u> specified in any of the sources, and thus the option of whether or not the scop and alekeeper drink should be left to the symbelgifa and other symbelers.

The Symbel Rite

Symbel requires that the roles of the symbelgifa, scop, alekeeper, and þyle be filled. The symbelgifa should be the owner of the symbelhouse where the symbel is being held. If the symbel is held in a public place, then the most prominent person present should serve as symbelgifa. The scop should be a skilled poet with a good grasp of our legends and lore. If no one with such skill is present, then whoever has the most knowledge of our myths may serve as "scop". The alekeeper would be filled by a woman close to the symbelgifa (wife, sister, mother, girlfriend, and so on) or another woman of prominence. Like the scop, the þyle should be someone with a good knowledge of our lore, though his skill in poetry does not have to be of a scop's level. The þyle should also be someone with a working knowledge of modern heathendom and the persons in it, and, perhaps most importantly, he should have quite a bit of common sense.

The seating at symbel should place the symbelgifa at the head of the table, with those of most importance closest to him and those of lesser importance farther away. The alekeeper should be given a seat near the symbelgifa. The scop may be seated at the table or at a place where he may be best heard. It is up to the symbelgifa or a general consensus of the symbelers whether or not the scop and alekeeper drink.

Below is a formula for the rite:

I. Halllowing--This is an optional step that may be done away with. If it is included, the symbelgifa should perform a suitable rite to set the room apart as holy and prevent the intrusion of troublesome wights, such as the Old English charm *Siþ Gealdor* or the hammer working.

II. Forespeach--At this point the symbelgifa should open the symbel with a suitable speech. This speech should be something that will invoke the past and present as they exist in the minds of the participants for the proper mood of symbelness to begin. Though it appears in the middle of the second *Béowulf* symbel, I sometimes use a paraphrase of lines 489-490. I feel it invokes the past and present quite well.

Sit now to symbel and unseal they mettes

30

Sige's rethe say as thy soul whets.

While the above quote is in modern English, it may be said in Old English or even translated into Old Norse.

III. Pouring--This stage is actually concurrent with stage IV (the mynes). The alekeeper pours the initial drink for each symbeler in turn. As she does so she should make a statement to each participant, perhaps in alliterative verse. In each case the statement should never be demeaning or insulting. Following the pouring the alekeeper and her assistants fill the cup as needed.

IV. Mynes--At this point the myne drinks are drank. The symbelgifa begins the round and the mynes proceed in a sunwise fashion until all have made a myne drink. There is no limit to the number of mynes that may be made and it is up to the symbelgifa and the majority of the symbelers to decide when enough have been made. Regardless, the major gods (Wóden, Þunor, Fríge, Fréa, Fréo, Tíw, and so on) should have mynes drank to them, as should any important forebears. The gods are always drank to first, then the forebears, then the living.

V. Gift Giving--Gifts are now exchanged between the participants of the symbel. The gift giving should begin with the symbelgifa, then proceed according to importance. Not every symbel must include the giving of gifts, so this should be left to the occasion.

VI. Léoð--At this point the scop recites a léoð. The léoð may be a myth from the Eddas or the recounting of a more recent event in the past. The léoð's entire purpose is to link the symbelers with the past so that they may affect the flow of wyrd.

VII. Gielps and béots--The symbelers then proceed to make the gielps and béots. The symbelgifa begins the round of gielps, then it proceeds according to importance. Each participant may wish to end his béot as Béowulf did his first one, "Goeth ever Wyrd as she shall."

Once a béot is made, the symbelgifa may accept or reject it (in which case it is not binding), then the þyle may challenge the béot. The þyle should not make challenges without justification, and should always base his challenge on valid facts, not on his own personal opinion. In other words, challenges should be made only if here is more than a reasonable doubt that the previous symbeler might not keep his béot. The risk involved in making a challenge is aptly portrayed in *Béowulf*, where in Béowulf's reply to Unferð's challenge it is revealed that Unferð killed his kinsmen.

If a challenge is made, the participant who made the béot gets to reply. The reply should in some way reinforce the béot, and discredit any fallacies the þyle may have stated. The symbelgifa then weighs the béot, the challenge, and the reply and either accepts or rejects the béot.

Once the first round of gielps and béots has been made, the scop recites another léoð and a new round of gielps and béots begins. This cycle may continue as long as the symbelgifa, scop and alekeeper see fit, though if the majority of symbelers want to quit it may end there.

VIII. Endspeech--Once the symbel has reached its end, the symbelgifa should utter a suitable closing statement or "endspeech".

Suggestions for Symbel

Above all else, the state of symbelness must be preserved. For that reason, many considerations must be made when holding symbel. The most obvious of these is the question of interruptions at symbel. As shown in *Béowulf*, people can and did enter symbel after it had begun and leave before it had ended. Given the sometimes busy schedules of people today, there is no reason modern heathen cannot permit this as well. It must be stressed, however, that such comings and goings should be kept as quiet and as unobtrusive as possible, so as not to disrupt the mood of symbelness, which may not be easily achieved again. Similarly, if there is a landline phone in the symbelhouse, it should be placed off the hook and any mobile phones should be set on "silent" or turned off completely. Any electrical appliances (such as TV sets, dryers, and so on) beyond air conditioners and fans (necessary in many places in the summer) should be shut off.

To further prevent any disruptions of symbelness, the symbelgifa, scop, and alekeeper should actively discourage any antagonism within the symbel. No harsh words should be uttered between the participants, and even the ritualised challenges should be worded as diplomatically as possible. Symbel is no different from any other rite in that frith, above all else, must prevail.

Finally, considerations must be made concerning the use of alcohol. While mead, beer, and ale are the traditional drinks of symbel, they should not be served to alcoholics, underage drinkers, or pregnant women. For these participants non-alcoholic drinks of a traditional nature (such as sweet cider) should be provided.

The more immediate effects of the symbel ale must also be accounted for. Symbel is an occasion to influence one's wyrd, not to get falling down drunk. If at any point it appears someone had had too much to drink, the symbel should end right then and there. Better to end the symbel while symbelness is still high than to have it disrupted by someone acting like a fool, vomiting, or passing out.

Finally, no one who has drunk at symbel should be allowed to drive himself home. To prevent any instance of drunk driving the symbelgifa, scop, or alekeeper should see that sleeping arrangements are made so symbelers can spend the night, or see to it that rides home are provided. If the scop or the alekeeper have not drunk during the ritual, they would be ideal to drive symbelers home. The memory of a good symbel should not be marred by accidents brought on by too much alcohol.

Symbel is perhaps the most important rite a heathen can take part in. For that reason it should be approached with a sense of frith, solemnity, and, yes, festivity. If a symbel goes well, then its participants may expect much happiness to come.

Symbel Wordhoard

alekeeper: The chief dispenser of drink at symbel.
béot: (OE) A "boast" with the binding force of an oath
endspeech: (OE *ende-spræc*) an epilogue or closing statement.
forespeech: (OE *forespræc*) A prologue or opening statement.

hallowing: The setting apart of an area as holy.

mette: (OE *meot*) dream, thought.

myne: (OE) memory, remembrance (as in myne drink).

rethe: (OE *hreð*) Glory.

scop: (OE) An official poet, attached to a lord, in charge of eulogising the lord and his forebears.

sige: (OE) Victory.

symbelgifa: (OE) Literally, giver of symbels.

symbelhouse: (OE *symbelhús*) A building in which a symbel is held.

yare: (OE *gearo*) Ready, prepared.

gielp: (OE) A boast retelling the past deeds of one's forebears or oneself. In symbel, made before a béot.

Bookhoard

1. Bauschatz, Paul. *The Well and the Tree.* Amherst, MA: University of Massachusetts Press, 1982.

2. Chishlm, James (trs.), "The Flyting of Loki", *Idunna*, March 1993, Austin, TX: Ring of Troth.

3. Conquergood, Dwight, "Literacy and Oral Performance in Anglo-Saxon England: Conflict and Confluence of Traditions," Annadale, Virginia Speech Communication Association.

4. Glosecki, Stephen. *Shamanism and Old English Poetry*, New York: Garland Publishing, 1990.

5. Klaeber, Fr. *Béowulf*, Lexington, MA: D.C. Heath and Co., 1950.

6. Opland, Jeff. *Anglo-Saxon Oral Poetry: a Study of the Traditions*. New York: Yale\ University Press, 1980.

Vatni Ausa and Nafn Gefa

Birth Rituals in Ancient Heathendom

Introduction

Rituals surrounding the birth of a child can be found in many cultures through the ages. For modern individuals perhaps the most familiar such rituals are the Christian christening ceremony or the Jewish circumcision ceremony. Given the widespread practice of rituals at or shortly after birth, it would seem likely that such rituals were practised among the ancient Germanic peoples. Unfortunately, little information has survived with regards to the possible rituals surrounding the birth of a child among the ancient Germanic peoples. In many cases we only have a few tantalising scraps regarding the rites that may have taken place during or upon the birth of a child.

Rites at Birth

We have next to no information as to what rites if any, might have taken place during childbirth. Two poems indicate that prayers to various gods played a role during the birth of a child.

Sigdrífumál verse 9 states:
Help runes you shall know

if you will help
and loose a child from a woman;
in the palm of the hand you shall write them
and grasp at the wrists
and pray to the Dísir for aid.

From *Sigdrífumál* it would appear that runes were sometimes
used to aid in childbirth. This should come as no surprise, as
both runes and gealdors were used to heal individuals in the
days of yore. In *Egils Saga* Egil cured a girl of her illness using
both runes and a gealdor. And the vast majority of Old English
gealdors deal in healing.

In *Oddrúnargráttr*, verse 10 is to be spoken to aid in childbirth:
So may the holy wights
help you,
Frigg and Freyja
and more gods yet,
as you have saved me
from peril.

This verse is obviously a prayer calling upon the "holy wights",
Frigg and Freyja, and yet more gods. It is impossible to say
who the "holy wights" are, although given *Sigdrífumál* it seems
possible that they could be the Dísir and similar wights.

If both *Sigdrífumál* and *Oddrúnargráttr* are any indication, it
appears that prayers were made as birth was taking place. In
both cases either the Dísir, or the "holy wights", Frigg and
Freyja, and other gods are called upon to aid in the birth of a
child.

It appears that in the case of a very difficult birth, other
measures might be taken. *Flateyjárbók* tells how Olaf II's

mother was having difficulty giving birth to him. A belt, a gold ring, and a sword were then taken from the burial mound of Olaf Geirstaðaálfr. Perhaps because of this, people apparently thought he was Olaf Geirstaðaálfr reborn. *Flateyjárbók* tells a story about Olaf II and his bodyguard riding past the burial mound of Olaf Geirstaðaálfr. His bodyguard asked Olaf II if he had ever been buried in the mound. Olaf II strenuously denied this.

On the surface it would appear that the people believed Olaf II to literally be the reincarnation of Olaf Geirstaðaálfr; that is, Olaf Geirstaðaálfr's resided in Olaf II's body. This might not necessarily be the case, however, as borne out by Edred Thorsson's article "Is Sigurðr Sigmundr 'aptrborinn'". In the article Thorsson discusses the concept of *aptrburðr* (a noun reconstructed from the Old Norse past participle *aptrborinn*). According to Thorsson, in the process of *aptrburðr, the hamingja and fylgja are passed down from an ancestor to a descendent.[1] It seems possible, then, that when Olaf II was said to be Olaf Geirstaðaálfr "aptrborinn", it was simply an indication that he had inherited the hamingja and fygja of his ancestor, Olaf Geirstaðaálfr.

At least in the case of difficult births, it would then seem that a child was given objects belonging to an ancestor. Perhaps it was hoped that the particular ancestor to whom the objects belonged would aid in the birth. It seems likely that it was hoped that the hamingja and fylgja of the ancestor would be passed to the child.

Both *Sigdrífumál* and *Oddrúnargráttr* indicate that prayers may have played a role in the birth of a child. *Sigdrífumál* indicates that runes may have been used to help with birth. In extremely difficult births, as that of Olaf II, it seems that objects belonging to an ancestor were given to the unborn child. Little more exists in the lore as to what rituals might have taken place at birth. It seems that the most important rites took place sometime after the child was born.

Presenting the Child, Vatni Ausa, and Nafna Gefa

While there is little information on the rituals that may have taken place at birth, there is actually a good deal of information on rituals following the birth of a child. *Hákonar Saga goða* tells how Earl Sigurðr's wife presented their son to King Hakon. Hakon approved of the boy. sprinkled him with water, and gave him his own name. In *Volsunga Saga*, Sigurðr Volsung was presented to King Hjálprekr, and then sprinkled with water and given the name "Sigurðr". From these sources it would appear that this ritual following the birth of a child consisted of three parts: 1. Presenting the child to either the local chieftain or the child's father; 2. Sprinkling the child with water (in Old Norse *vatni aussa*); and 3. Giving a name to the child.

The presentation of a child to his father or a local chieftain would appear to give his father or the local chieftain the opportunity to approve the child, thus insuring his acceptance in both his kindred and the local community. According to Thorsson, if a child was not accepted by his father or a local chieftain, he could then be exposed or left out to die. If the child was killed, then the child's wergild would then only be that of an unborn child (which was a mere fifth of that for other children).[2] When a father or local chieftain accepted a child presented to him. it seems that the child was not only considered part of the family and part of the community, but that it was considered fully human--with all the rights that entails.

The second part of the rite is usually called *vatni ausa*, literally "to sprinkle with water". References to *vatni ausa* occur in both the *Poetic Edda* and the Icelandic sagas. *Hávamál* verse 158 reads:
A thirteenth I know:
if I shall upon a young thegn
throw water,
he shall not fall,
although he fares to battle,
nor will he sink beneath swords.

Rigsþula refers to *vatni ausa* no less than three times:

Rigsþula 7
Edda bore a child,
they sprinkled him with water,
the swarthy one,
and called him Þræl.

Rigsþula 20-21
…Amma bore a child,
sprinkled him with water,
called him Karl,
the woman wrapped him in a linen jerkin,

ruddy and redhaired,
with flashing eyes.

Rigsþula 33
A boy bore Móðir,
wrapped him in silk,

sprinkled him with water,
and named him Jarl.

In the Sagas *vatni ausa* is mentioned so frequently that quoting every single instance would occupy a good part of this article. Besides the examples above from *Hákonar Saga goða* and *Volusnga Saga*, it also appears in *Njals Saga*, *Eyrbyggja Sata*, and *Egils Saga* among others.

Eyrbyggja Saga reads:
"Þórsteinn Þorskabítur had a son who was called Börkr the Stout. But in the summer when Þórsteinn was a half thirty years old, Þóra bore him a boy child who was named Grímur and who was sprinkled with water. That boy Þórsteinn gave to Þórr, and said that he should be a hofgoði and called him Þórgrim."

Egils Saga reads:
"Þóra had a baby in the summer, and it was a girl; she was sprinkled with water and given the name Ásgerðr."

The phrase *vatni ausa* occurs often enough that it may well have been a formula used in the rite ("I sprinkle you with water and name you…," for example). In some cases the phrase *verpa vatni*, "to throw water" is used (an example is *Hávamál* verse 158), although the meaning would essentially be the same. Water was either sprinkled or thrown on the child who was about to be named.[3]

Thorsson theorises that the *vatni ausa* appears "to be a ritual for the (re)-integration of a child into the stream of organic life."[4] There could be another purpose behind the *vatni ausa* portion of the rite, however. In *The Well and the Tree* Paul C. Bauschatz theorises that the water of Urðarbrunnr, the Well of

Wyrd, are the past actions of all wights who exist within the worlds. [5] It might not be far-fetched to believe that the water used in the *vatni ausa* part of the rite was thought to symbolise the water from the Well of Wyrd. If that was the case, then sprinkling a child with water could be a means of connecting him with the past actions of his family, of his community, and the worlds. In effect, it could be a means of integrating the child into the flow of wyrd.

Some might be tempted to believe that *vatni ausa* could have been borrowed from the Christian christening rite. It seems likely that such individuals could be wrong. Portions of the *Hávamál* appear to go as far back as the 10th Century, making many of its verses among the oldest found in the *Poetic Edda*. In other words, we could have reference to *vatni ausa* well before Christianity had a foothold in the north. Beyond this, there is also the fact that in Old Norse and Icelandic *vatni ausa* is <u>never</u> used of Christian christening. The term for christening in both Old Norse and Icleandic was *scíra* "to cleanse, to purify". If *vatni ausa* developed from Christian christening, it seems unlikely that two different terms would be used for the two rituals.

As seen in the examples above, the *vatni ausa* rite or "sprinkling with water" is always accompanied by giving a name to the child. Beyond giving the child a name he can be called by, the *nafn gefa* ("to give a name") portion of the rite would appear to be the final step in making the child part of the family and part of the community. Indeed, Germanic naming practices would seem to emphasise the connection of individuals with the ancestors who had preceded them. As pointed out above, Olaf II was named for his ancestor Olaf Geirstaðaálfr. In *Sturlunga Saga* Kolbeinn Arnorson was named for his uncle Kolbeinn Túmason. Even when a whole name was not used particular words might be passed down family lines. Probably the most obvious example of this can be found among the Volsungs. The prefix *Sig-* appears in the names of father and son *Sigmundr* and *Sigurðr*. Among the Frankish kings, the prefix *Chlod-* appears repeatedly. It appears in the name of King Chlodovech (better known as Clovis I), his son *Chlodomer* (also known as Gondieuque), and his son Chlodovald (also known as St. Cloud).[6]

Besides showing that a child belonged to a particular family, naming a child for an ancestor or using a particular prefix in the names of family member repeatedly through the years could have been done to encourage the passage of the hamingja and fylgja to a child. Indeed, from the example from *Flateyjárbók* cited above, this would seem to be the case in Olaf II being named for Olaf Geristaðaálfr.

From various sources, it would then appear that a three part ritual was performed shortly after the child's birth. The child was presented to his father or a chieftain to determine if he would be accepted into the kindred and the community. The child was sprinkled with water, perhaps to integrate him into the flow of life or to link him to the past of his kindred and community. Finally, the child was given a name, usually one that would link him to his ancestors and thus encourage the passage of hamingja and fylgja from an ancestor to a child.

Conclusion

The birth of a child is among the most important events in the life of an individual and even a family. That the ancient sources how that prayers may have been conducted during birth and the presentation/*vatni ausa*/*nafn gefa* rite was performed not long after birth show that the Old Norse speakers realised this

43

importance. For modern heathen, then, there is little reason we should not readopt some of these traditions.

Footnotes

1. Thorsson, Edred. "Is Sigurðr Sigmundr 'aptrborinn'", *Idunna*, volume 4, issue 1, March 1992, pp. 6--12.
2. *ibid.*
3. Thorsson, Edred. "Is Sigurðr Sigmundr 'aptrborinn'", *Idunna*, volume 4, issue 1, March 1992, p. 12.
4. Thorsson, Edred. "Is Sigurðr Sigmundr 'aptrborinn'", *Idunna*, volume 4, issue 1, March 1992, p, 9.
5. Bauschatz, Paul C. *The Well and the Tree*, pp. 19-21.
5, Thorsson, Edred. "Is Sigurðr Sigmundr 'aptrborinn'", *Idunna*, volume 4, issue 1, March 1992, p. 7.

Wordhoard

fylgja: An Old Norse word that in some sagas would seem to indicate a guardian spirit attached to a particular individual.

hamingja: An Old Norse word that was used of "luck" and seems to have referred to some metaphysical force.

nafn gefa: In Old Norse, literally, to give a name.

vatni ausa: In Old Norse, literally, to sprinkle with water.

Bookhoard

Baschatz, Paul C. *The Well and the Tree*. The University of Massachusetts Press, Amherst, MA 1982.

Cleasby, Richard. Vigfusson, Gudbrand (eds.). *An Icelandic-English Dictionary*. Oxford. Clarendon Press. 1975

Ellis, Davidson, H. R. "The Sword at the Wedding", *Folklore*, Volume 71, March 1960, pp. 1-18.

Thorsson, Edred. "Is Sigurðr Sigmundr 'aptrborinn'", *Idunna*, volume 4, issue 1, March 1992, pp. 6--13.

Turvllle-Petre, E. O. G., *Myth and Religion of the North*. New York; Holt, Reinheart, and Winston, 1964

Bride Prices and Bridals:
Heathen Weddings

Marriage Among the Early Germanic Peoples

As hard as it is to believe, very little information survives on how individuals among the ancient Germanic peoples got married. We know about many of the arrangements that were made before the wedding. We even know some of the customs that might be practised after a wedding. But nowhere does a complete wedding ceremony appear in any of the ancient sources for any of the ancient Germanic peoples. This leaves modern heathen at a bit of a loss. How does one perform a traditional wedding? The answers is that perhaps we cannot, but by researching the lore we can at least come as close as humanly possible.

The earliest reference to marriage among the ancient Germanic peoples occurs in Tacitus' *Germania*. Tacitus explains that the groom gives the bride a dowry. The parents and kin of the bride and groom approve the gifts. Typical gifts include oxen, a horse and bridle, a shield, a spear, and sword. The exchange of gifts is essential to the holy bonds of marriage. Following the exchange of gifts, holy rituals to sanctify the marriage under the auspices of the gods of marriage are held. According to Tacitus, the wedding ritual reminds the bride that she is entering her husband's home to share in work and the perils that occur during both peace and war. The bride is expected to hand down the gifts she receives upon marriage to her children, so that they might pass them on to their wives and hence to her grandchildren.

Tacitus's description of marriage among the early Germanic peoples is amazingly consistent with that seen among later Germanic peoples, such as the Anglo-Saxons and the Scandinavians. Among the features in Tacitus's description found among the Germanic peoples in later eras is the giving of gifts. Tacitus indicates that the exchange of gifts was central to the bonds of marriage. And it does not appear he was wrong. Among the Germanic peoples it was believed that the giving of gifts created a bond between two people. In the groom giving gifts to the bride and vice versa, the two of them are then forging bonds between themselves.[1]

Old Norse sources refer to another feature found in Tacitus, that of hallowing the marriage under the blessing of the marriage gods. It would seem that the Old Norse speakers believed it wise to call upon the gods in the beginning of a marriage, much as the Germanic peoples of the First Century CE did.

Overall, Tacitus's description of marriage among the Germanic peoples agrees with that found among the Anglo-Saxons and the Scandinavian peoples of the Viking Age so much that it might not be too foolish to assume that marriage customs varied but little among the early Germanic peoples of any era. As will be seen below, customs Tacitus described were still being practised in the early Dark Ages and the Viking Era.

Marriage Among the Anglo-Saxon Peoples

Anglo-Saxon marriage appears to have differed but little from that found among the Germanic peoples described in Tacitus' *Germania*. A man would meet with the family of the woman he wished to marry with a proposal of marriage. He would usually

47

be accompanied by his most prestigious kinfolk or friends, who would help in negotiations and could demonstrate the power and prestige the man could bring to the marriage. Provided the proposal was not rejected by the woman's family and the woman herself, negotiations regarding the amount of the *brýdcéap* (literally "bride price") would begin. The brýdcéap consisted of three payments--the *handgeld* or *mund*, the *morgengifu*, and the *brýdgifu*. The agreement would be sealed by a handshake, wich the groom's kin or friends would witness.

As part of his brýdcéap, the groom was expected to make two payments. The first was called the handgeld or mund. It seems to have had a threefold purpose. The first was to pay the bride's family for the right of guardianship and protection. Put more simply, the payment of the mund would officially make the bride part of the groom's family. The second was perhaps to reimburse the bride's family for the loss of labour that would occur when she married. Finally, the mund might have been a means of demonstrating the groom's ability to support his new wife. The mund would usually be paid at the wedding ceremony. The second payment the groom was expected to make was the morgengifu or "morning gift". This was paid the morning following the wedding night. Its purpose appears to have been to insure the wife's continued financial support throughout the marriage.

While the groom was expected to pay the mund and morgengifu, the bride's family was expected to pay the brýdgifu (literally "bride gift"). The brýdgifu was kept by the bride and could not be touched by the groom. In the event of her husband's death or divorce, it remained hers to keep. Its purpose appears to have been to insure that the wife and her children would remain financially supported regardless of what circumstances might befall her.

48

Unfortunately, we know very little about Anglo-Saxon wedding ceremonies. The ceremony apparently started with the procession of the bride and her family to the spot where the weding would take place, the procession being called the *brýdhlóp* in Old English. Afterwards the *brýdeala* (literally "bride's ale", our modern word *bridal*) would take place. The brýdeala could be termed a "wedding feast", although it seems likely that boasts of the sort made at symbel were probably made. Once the wedding night had taken place, the groom paid the morgengifu.

As can be seen above, Anglo-Saxon marriage resembles the outline of marriage among the early Germanic peoples provided by Tacitus in *Germania* to a large degree. Like marriage among the early Germanic peoples, the exchange of gifts appears to have been central to marriage. Whatever other purposes the exchange of gifts might have had, it is safe to assume that among the Anglo-Saxons, just as among other Germanic peoples, it was meant to create a bond between the bride and groom, as well as a bond between the bride's family and the groom's family.

Marriage Among the Scandinavians of the Viking Era

Marriages among the Scandinavians of the Viking Era resemble marriages among the early Germanic peoples and the Anglo-Saxons to a large degree. A major difference from marriages among the Anglo-Saxons is that marriages among the Scandinavians of the Viking Age appear to have been largely arranged by the families involved. It is unclear to how much say a man had in choosing the woman he wished to marry. Gunnora Hallakarva points out that it could be that it was assumed that the man's consent was required prior to negotiations, although it is possible that he had no say in the

49

matter whatsoever.[2] What is clear that women *legally* had no say in consenting to a marriage, a right which belonged to their legal guardians. A woman's legal guardian was most often her father, although it could be a brother or other kinsman if her father was dead. While legally women had no right to choose their husbands, families often found it wise to get their approval of any prospective marriages. The sagas show that marriages made without the bride's consent often ended in disaster.[3]

Much like marriages among the Anglo-Saxon peoples, marriages mong the Viking Age Scandinavians began with negotiations. A man or more often his family would approach the family of an eligible woman with a proposal. They would usually be accompanied by powerful acquaintances who could act as advocates or brokers throughout the process. Provided the proposal of marriage was accepted the amount of the *brúðkaup* (literally "bride price") would be negotiated. As among the Anglo-Saxons, the brúðkaup consisted of three payments: the *mundr*, the *morginngjöf*, and the heimanfylgja. And just as among the Anglo-Saxons, the agreement would be sealed with a handshake witnessed by the groom's powerful acquaintances.[4]

The bride's family was expected to pay the *heimanfylgia*. The heimanfylgia was the equivalent of the Anglo-Saxon *brýdgifu*. It could not be confiscated to pay the husband's debts nor could it be confiscated with the husband's goods should he be outlawed. In the event of the husband's death or divorce, the heimanfylgia would be kept by the wife.[6]

According to *An Icelandic-English Dictionary*, the marriage contract, including the agreed upon brúðkaup, was read at the wedding feast or *brullaup*. The word *brullaup* appears to have originally been *brúðhlaup*, precisely the same word as Old

50

Engilsh *brúðhlóp*. It may have originally referred to the bridal procession, although in the sources it is only used of the bridal feast itself.[7]

Complete descriptions of the bridal feast or brullaup are difficult to find in Old Norse and Icelandic sources. Perhaps the two best are a description of a bridal feast in *Bósa saga og Herraud* and the Eddic poem *Þrymskviða*. In *Bósa saga og Herraud* it is told how Bósi and Herraud attended a brullaup held by King Godmund. There it is told how the important guests were shown to their seats and the bride was led to her seat of honour by a large number of young women. A minstrel played the harp during the toasts. The first toast appears to have been a minni to Þórr. It was at this point that the minstrel played so well that many people rose from their seats to dance.

A toast to all the gods followed, at which point the minstrel changed the tune and everyone but the king, the bride, and the groom got up to dance. After the minstrel played some more songs, the toast to Óðinn was drank. The minstrel played yet more and everyone danced. The final toast, one to Freyja, was then made. After this there was yet more dancing...

In the poem *Þrymskviða*, the ettin Þrym stole Þórr's hammer and would return it only if he could receive Freyja's hand in marriage. Since Freyja absolutely refused to go through with such a marriage, Þórr, disguised as Freyja, would go in her place. Accompanied by Loki, who was disguised as a lady in waiting, the two rode to the home of Þrym. Þrym prepared a huge feast of an ox, eight salmon, and three measures of mead. Þrym asked why "Freyja (in reality Þórr) ate so much and the lady in waiting (in reality Loki) replied that she had not eaten for eight nights. When Þrym asked why "Freyja's" eyes were so red, Loki replied that she had not slept in eight nights. The ettin's sister then asked for a brúðfé, presumably the

51

heimanfylgja, to be paid by the bride's family. Þrym finally announced that the hammer should be brought out to hallow the bride. The hammer was placed in "Freyja's" lap, at which point Þórr killed every last ettin.

In both *Bósa saga og Herraud* and *Þrymskviða*, it would seem that a bridal procession of some sort took place. In *Bósa saga og Herraud* we are told that many young women led the bride into the hall. In *Þrymskviða* it is simply Þórr and Loki who make the journey to Þrym's home. The bridal procession in Old Norse was called the *brúðargang*. As indicated by *Bósa saga og Herraud*, the maidens and ladies came in first, then at last would come the bride--the central woman in the wedding. It appears that the groom also had his own journey to make. The groom was expected to meet his guests a fourth of a mile from his house. Come evening, they would ride home two by two. This ride was called the *brúðgumareið*, the "bridegroom's ride".[8]

In *Bósa saga og Herraud* we are told that once the bride was seated, the toasts were made. Toasts were drunk to Þórr, all the gods, Óðinn, and Freyja. It seems like that these toasts were meant to attract the attention of the gods and hence insure that they would place their blessings upon the union. Curiously, Old Norse and Icelandic sources do not mention blóts to the gods being made in conjunction with weddings. It seems likely that they may have been. In *Germania* Tacitus stated that marriages were sanctified under the blessings of the gods. Writing nearly 1000 years, Adam of Bremen stated, in *The Deeds of the Bishops of the Church of Hamburg*, that for weddings the Swedes made offerings to Freyr. It then seems quite possible that Scandinavians of the Viking Age held a blót in conjunction with weddings to insure the gods' blessings.

The description of the brullaup in *Bósa saga og Herraud* makes it sound as if the minstrel played and the people danced even as toasts were being made. To many readers, and this author as well, this might not sound like the best of situations. At best the music and dancing would seem to distract from the toasts to the gods. At worst it would seem to be downright disrespectful to the gods being toasted. It should be noted that in the symbels portrayed in *Béowulf*, the rounds of béots and geilps rotate with poems sang by the scop. At no point does the scop appear to be singing a poem while a béot and gielp is being spoken.[9] Symbel being a very similar rite to a brullaup, it seems likely that the minstrel played and the folk danced in between rounds of toasts.

The ceremonial drinking that took place at the brullaup was very important in Viking Age Scandinavia. In fact, under the laws of Viking Age Norway, the bride and groom were required to drink together for the marriage to be vaild.[10]

Þrymskviða makes no mention of toasts to the gods, but it does refer to the hallowing of the bride with the hammer (in this case the hammer--Þórr's Mjölnir). This is not the only instance in which a hammer is used for hallowing. In the *Prose Edda* Snorri states that Þórr hallowed Baldr's balefire with Mjölnir. It must be noted that a number of memorial stones in Scandinavia dating to the Viking Age bear an inscription of a hammer with the words *Þur viki* "May Þórr hallow..."[11]

Like the brullaup, the laws of Viking Age Norway also regulated the activities of the wedding night. According to Gragas, the groom must be placed in bed with the bride "by light" by at least six legal witnesses. Gunnora Hallkarva states that it is unclear whether the phrase "by light" means the groom and bride must be placed in bed by daylight or they must be placed in bed by torchlight. She concludes that since the day would have most likely been occupied by feasting and drinking, the bedding would probably take place after dark and hence by torchlight. Regardless, the purpose of witnesses leading the groom to bed would seem to be to guarantee that the marriage was consummated. The witness could identify the bride and groom if any question of the marriage's validity arose.[12]

As can be seen above, weddings in Scandinavia during the Viking Era largely resembled those found among the Germanic peoples of the first century as well as the Anglo-Saxons. Gift giving was central to the marriage in all the cases. In fact, the exchange of gifts involved in Scandinavian marriages parallel those of Anglo-Saxon marriages (mund/handgeld or mund, morginngjöf/morgengifu, heimanfylgia/brýdgifu). The resemblances between Scandinavian weddings and Anglo-Saxon weddings go even further than this. In both cases ritual drinking plays a large role--the Anglo-Saxon brýdeala and the Scandinavian brullaup. It would seem that when it came to marriage customs, the Germanic peoples were not only very consistent, but very conservative. A first century Germanic tribesman would not feel out of place at an Anglo-Saxon or Viking wedding.

Modern Day Heathen Weddings

The similarity between Anglo-Saxon weddings and Scandinavian weddings of the Viking Era makes it possible to create an outline of a wedding ceremony that modern day heathen wishing for a somewhat traditional wedding could use. Here then is an outline of a heathen wedding ceremony.

1. Negotiations: Today most women can support themselves, but negotiating a brýdcéap or brúðkaup had another, perhaps more important purpose than insuring the bride's financial stability in times to come. Through the exchange of gifts a bond was forged between the bride and groom. For modern day heathen couples wishing to create such a bond between themselves, the exchange of gifts would then seem to be a wise idea. The a brýdcéap or brúðkaup should be composed of the three payments to be made: the mundr or handgeld initially paid by the groom to the bride's family; the heimanfylgia or brýdgifu paid by the bride's family to the groom for the bride's use; and the morginngjöf or morgengifu paid by the groom to the bride.

In "The Sword At the Wedding" H. R. Ellis Davidson puts forth the theory that swords may have been a portion of the gifts exchanged between bride and groom at weddings. This may be borne out by Tacitus's statement in *Germania* that the bride's dowry usually included a sword, spear, and shield, which she would usually pass down to her children. It may also be borne out by the fact that a number of Germanic heroes received swords from their mothers or their mother's family (Grettir in *Grettis Saga*, Sigurðr in *Volsunga Saga*, Glúm in *Víga-Glúms Saga*). Davidson theorises that the family sword may have symbolised the continuation of the kinded. She also theorises that it may have been linked to the family's fylgja and the family luck. The gift of the sword would then both represent the continuation of the family, as well as passing the fylgja and family luck onto the bride and another generation.[13] Those who truly desire a traditional wedding might consider an exchange of swords between bride and groom.

2. Blót: It is unclear whether blóts were held in conjunction with weddings among the Anglo-Saxons and Viking Age Scandinavians. Given Tacitus's reference to holy rituals to sanctify the marriage under the auspices of the gods and Adam of Bremen's reference to the Swedes giving offerings to Freyr for weddings, it seems quite likely. It is unclear whether a

55

wedding blót would take place before or after the bridal procession; however it seems likely that it would take place before the brýdeala or brullaup. In *Hákonar Saga goða*, the blót (the slaying of animal for the gods in this case) took place before the feast. It would then seem that if a blót was performed in conjunction with a wedding, then it would take place before the bridal feast (the brýdeala or brullaup)

3. The Brýdhlóp or Brúðargang: This is the bridal procession. The bride's kinswomen and female friends lead the bride to the site of the wedding. Once within the hall, the bride should take her place in the seat of honour, after which the guests may be seated.

4. The Brúðgumareið: At the exact same time that the brýdhlóp or brúðargang takes place, a procession of the groom, his kinsmen, and male friends make their way to the site of the wedding. The procession should be two by two.

5. The Reading of the Contract: Once everyone is seated, the marriage contract is read before the wedding party.

6. Payment of the Handgeld or Mundr and the Brýdgifu or Heimanfylgia: It is at this point that the groom pays the handgeld or mundr to the bride's family and the bride's family pays the groom the brýdgifu or heimanfylgia.

It is unclear whether vows were ever exchanged in ancient Germanic weddings. Presumably they would have been part of the marriage contract, so that uttering them at the wedding would be superfluous. However, if the individuals wish to exchange vows at their wedding, this would be a suitable time for it.

7. Hallowing the Bride: At this point a hammer should be placed in the bride's lap to hallow her.

8. Brýdeala or Brullaup: The bridal feast then begins. The bride and groom should take their first drink together, following which the gathered folk should toast the couple. Toasts to the gods (Þunor, all of the gods, Wóden, and Freyja) would then follow. Between rounds of toasts, entertainment such as much and dancing would be permitted.

9. The Wedding Night: The groom and bride depart for their wedding bed. Under Anglo-Saxon custom, no witnesses were required to see the groom go to bed with the bride. Under ancient Norwegian law, however, witnesses were required for such. It is left up to individual Norse heathen whether they wish for witnesses to escort the groom to the wedding bed. ..

10. The Morgengifu or Morginngjóf: The next morning the groom gives the bride the morgengifu or morginngjóf before witnesses.

Endnotes

1. Wodening, Eric. *We Are Our Deeds*, p. 67.

2. Hallakarva, Gunnora. *Courtship, Love, and Marriage in Viking Scandinavia*. http://www.vikinganswerlady.com/wedding.htm
3. *ibid.*
4. *ibid.*
5. *ibid.*
6. *ibid.*
7. *An Icelandic-English Dictinoary*, p. 83.
9. Wodening, Eric. "An Anglo-Saxon Symbel", pp. 11-20. *Theod*, Wælburges 1995.
10. Hallakarva, Gunnora, *Courtship, Love, and Marriage in Viking Scandinavia*, http://www.vikinganswerlady.com/wedding.htm
11. Turville-Petre, E.O.G., p. 101.

12. Hallakarva, Gunnora, *Courtship, Love, and Marriage in Viking Scandinavia*, http://www.vikinganswerlady.com/wedding.htm

13. Ellis Davidson, H. R., "The Sword at the Wedding", *Folklore*, Volume 71, March 1960, pp. 1-18.

Cattle Die, Kinsmen Die
Funerals Among the Ancient Heathen

Funerals Among the Early Germanic Tribes

When it came to funerals, the Germanic peoples appear to have been rather conservative. A funeral held among the Germanic tribesmen of the 1st Century CE would look only a little different from a funeral held among Angles in the 6th Century England. A funeral held among Angles of 6th Century England would look only a little different from a funeral held among Norwegians of the 10th Century.

Perhaps the earliest reference to funeral practices among the Germanic peoples is in Tacitus's *Germania*. Tacitus states that their funerals are simple. They burn bodies of nobles with special kinds of wood. Sometimes they will place the man's armour and even his horse on the balefire, but they add neither his garments nor incense. They raise sod mounds in hour of the dead, but never monuments. Neither their tears nor their laments last long, although they continue to mourn. The women weep. The men remember.

From this very basic outline we see features found in later Germanic funerals. The body is often cremated. Goods are often placed on the pyre. A mound is raised in honour of the dead. These elements can be found in time slater than the 1st Century and in places other than the Continent. They can also be found in Anglo-Saxon England and Viking Age Scandinavia.

59

Funerals Among the Anglo-Saxons and Continental Saxons

For information on Anglo-Saxon funeral practices and perhaps even Germanic funeral practices in general, there is perhaps no better source than the poem *Beowulf*. Though it is often believed to have been written as late as the 8th Century and is often Christian in tone, the funerals portrayed in the poem seem undoubtedly heathen. Indeed, they are comparable to Tacitus's description of funerals among the early Germanic tries and funerals found in Old Norse and Icelandic sources as well.

The first funeral portrayed in *Beowulf* is that of Scyld Scefing, found in verse 26 to 62. Scyld Scefing had arrived in Denmark from over the sea as a child and later became king. When he died, his thegns carried him to the sea and placed him a ring prowed ship. They placed weapons, armour, and treasure aboard the ship alongside Scyld's body. They then gave Scyld's body, the ship, and the treasures aboard to the sea.

The second funeral portrayed in *Beowulf* is that of Hnæf, found in verses 1108 to 1123. Hnæf's body and those of many of his men were placed on the balefire, alongside ancient gold. Hildburh, Hnæf's sister, ordered her own son placed on the pyre at Hnæf's side. A woman lamented with songs. The smoke spiralled up into the sky. The fire roared. Heads melted. Wounds burst. And the balefire devoured all the slain.

By far the most detailed account of a funeral in *Beowulf* is that of Beowulf himself. It appears in verses 3112 to 3184. It tells how Wiglaf commanded everyone bring firewood from far and wide for the pyre on which Beowulf's body would be burned. He had seven of Beowulf's thegns gather treasure from the dragon's hoard (the dragon whom Beowulf had died slaying) to place on the pyre alongside Beowulf's corpse. At Hrones Ness they built the pyre on which to burn the body of Beowulf. They placed upon it helmets and other war gear. And then they placed Beowulf's body upon it. The balefire was then lit. The smoke rose and the flame roared, combined with the sound of weeping. The widow sounded her sorrow and mourned Beowulf's passing. When the balefire was over, the folk built a mound on the spot. It took ten days to raise it. In the mound they placed treasure. Then twelve athelings gathered about the barrow to mourn Beowulf. They sang songs. They spoke of Beowulf's leadership and his heroic deeds. They noted that Beowulf was the mildest, kindest, and most beloved of kings.

In addition to the funerals found in *Beowulf*, Widukind tells of a funeral held by the Continental Saxons after a victory in battle in *Deeds of the Saxons*. There Widukind tells how the Saxons held a funeral in honour of those slain after a victory. They gave praise to their slain leader as they "raised him to the sky." They hailed his virtues and his steadfastness that had led them to victory.

Using the funerals in *Beowulf*, one can create an outline of funerals as they might have been held among the Anglo-Saxon peoples. That the Continental Saxons might have had similar practices may be confirmed by Widukind's *Deeds of the Saxons*. In both Hnæf and Beowulf's funerals, funeral pyres were prepared. Upon these pyres were placed the bodies of the dead as well as treasure. While the bodies burned, a woman sang a funeral dirge or mourned. Although unmentioned in the description of Hnæf's funeral, the description of Beowulf's funeral tells how a mound was built, taking ten days. Upon the mound's completion, men gathered to sing Beowulf's praises. This reflects the description of a funeral held among the Continental Saxons in Widukind's *Deeds of the Saxons*.

61

It should be pointed out that while both Hnæf and Beowulf were cremated, burials were not uncommon among the Anglo-Saxon peoples. H. R. Ellis Davidson observes that it is probably not possible to set any hard and fast rules as to why some bodies were cremated and others buried. She points out that cremation is only possible where wood is plentiful. She also theorises that in Anglo-Saxon England it might have largely depended upon family custom as to whether bodies were cremated or buried.[1]

Regardless, there would appear to be ample evidence for funerals, such as that of *Beowulf*, in which the body was burned and the ashes then placed within a mound. There are graves from the Anglo-Saxon period in England in which the ashes were placed, usually in an urn. One such mound is to be found at Asthall in Oxfordshire. Even in the famous cemetery at Sutton Hoo, there were mounds built over cremation ashes.[2]

Evidence for funerals such as that of Scyld Scefing, in which a body was placed in a ship and set to sea, or even evidence for the well-known "Viking funeral", in which a body was cremated in a ship on the water, is not to be found. It seems possible that bodies were burned in ships among the Anglo-Saxons, as references are made to similar funerals among the Scandinavian peoples in Old Norse and Icelandic sources, as well as the Arab traveller Ibn Fadlan's account. Regardless, it seems apparent that the ship was significant in Anglo-Saxon funeral practices. The centrepiece of the famous Sutton Hoo burial was a large, sea-going ship. Smaller, less impressive ship burials have also been found in England. Another mound in the Sutton Hoo cemetery held another ship. At Snape, Suffolk, another smaller ship was found in a grave, as well as a burial in what appeared to be a small log boat.[3]

The description of Beowulf's funeral also makes reference to treasure being placed in the mound. This is also confirmed by archaeology. Perhaps the most famous example of goods being placed in a grave is that of the famous Sutton Hoo ship burial. Contained within the grave was a large ship, a purse holding Merovingian coins, an exquisite staff with a whetstone and a bronze stag at the top, well designed clasps for cloaks, a large gold buckle, and various weapons and armour. Other graves containing various goods have also been found. One grave contained a sword, three spears, a knife, a shield, and a spindle whorl. Another was found with a knife, a buckle, and a pair of drinking horns.[4]

It seems likely that the burning of bodies on ships found among the Scandinavians and the burial of bodies in ships found among the Anglo-Saxons and Scandinavians could have their roots in beliefs in the afterlife. It could be that such ships were expected to serve as vehicles to transport the dead to some afterworld (such as Valhöll mentioned in Old Norse and Icelandic sources). In Old English the word *forþfaran*, "to fare forth", was also used of death.[5] This shows that the Anglo-Saxons apparently saw death as the beginning of a journey. It seems possible that a belief in the afterlife might also be the reason why goods were placed on funeral pyres and in graves. It seems possible that the Germanic peoples believed the dead would use or need those items placed in their graves in their afterlives.

In *Beowulf*, once the mound was completed, it is told how men gathered to praise their fallen leader. This is not so different from the custom at Christian funerals, even those held to this day. It might then seem tempting to dismiss the athelings singing songs in honour of Beowulf as a Christian influence. This would not appear to be the case. First, there is Widukind's description of the Continental Saxons praising their fallen leader. Second, by singing praises to Beowulf, his athelings appear to have been engaging in something very similar to a ritual found in Old Norse and Icelandic sources--that of the *erfi* or *erfiöl* (our modern word *arval*), the so-called "funeral feast (see below)". The erfiöl appears to have been very similar to symbel, if not nearly the same. Drinking took place in rounds, with toasts to the dead man and apparently the gods as well (see below).

It is difficult to determine if a rite similar to the Norse erfiöl was shared by the Anglo-Saxons, although it does seem possible. The 10th Century archbishop Ælfric actually forbade his clergy from rejoicing upon a death, attending upon a corpse, engaging in heathen songs, and eating and drinking in the presence of a corpse. This could indicate that not only did the "funeral feast" exist among the Anglo-Saxons, but Anglo-Saxon Christians regarded it as a heathen rather than Christian custom. The possibility that a rite similar to the Norse erfiöl existed among the Anglo-Saxons maybe confirmed by one of the senses *A Concise Anglo-Saxon Dictionary* gives for the Old English verb *yrfan*, "to honour with a funeral feast." Unfortunately, it seems possible that this sense of *yrfan* could have been borrowed from the Old Norse verb *erfa*, "to honour with a funeral feast," "to inherit." In fact, it seems possible that the sort of eating and drinking that followed a death among the Anglo-Saxons which Ælfric condemned could have been borrowed from the Danes. In that case, it might not have been a ritual native to the Anglo-Saxon heathen. It could then hardly be regarded as an Anglo-Saxon heathen custom.

Regardless, it ultimately seems quite likely that the Anglo-Saxons did practise a ritual similar to the Norse erfiöl following a death. Besides Ælfric's condemnation of such practices, it should also be pointed out that there is a good deal of consistency between the Anglo-Saxon and Norse customs with regards to the various rituals dealing with life passages. For instance, both celebrated marriages with feasts (the Anglo-Saxon *brýdeala* and the Old Norse *brullaup*). It then seems possible that both honoured the dead with feasts. At any rate, the custom of the "funeral feast" is one known from the medieval era even up into the 16th Century. Individuals would set aside money so that people could "drink to their souls".[6]

From Ælfric's condemnation of such customs, it would appear that the "funeral feast" took place before the cremation or burial, with the corpse present at the "feast". This appears to be the opposite of the order in which it took place among the Scandinavians, in which the erfiöl also took place after the cremation or burial. It would also seem to run counter to the account of Beowulf's funeral. It is only after Beowulf's body is cremated and his ashes placed in a mound that the nobility gather to sing his praises.

Funerals Among the Scandinavians of the Viking Era

The Old Norse and Icelandic sources contain no accounts of funerals as detailed as that of Bewoulf's funeral. Still, there appears to be enough information scattered throughout the Old Norse and Icelandic sources to roughly reconstruct what a funeral among the Scandinavians of the Viking Age must have been like. To aid in this there is also the eye witness accounts of Arab travellers among the Rus, which can also add somewhat to our knowledge of Viking Age funerary practices.

Laxdæla Saga shows that funerals among the Viking Age Scandinavians may have proceeded in much the same fashion as that of Beowulf's funeral. According to *Laxdæla Saga*, when Höskuldr died, the people mourned terribly. A very fine mound was made for him, although little in the way of goods was placed in it. Höskuldr's sons decided to hold an erfiöl for him. Even though Höskuldr had died in the autumn, it was decided to hold his erfiöl in the summer so that people would not have difficulty in travelling. Höskuldr's erfiöl proved to be one of the most attended in the history of Iceland. There were nearly 900 guests. The funerals portrayed in *Gísla Saga* also follow a similar order. The deceased is interred in a mound, followed by the erfiöl afterwards. The only major difference between *Laxdæla Saga* and *Gísla Saga* is that the erfiöl took place several months after the burial, while in *Gísla Saga* the erfiöls took place immediately following the interment.

Despite the accounts in both *Laxdæla Saga* and *Gísla Saga*, the erfiöl does not always follow burial or cremation in Icelandic sources. In one of the *Fornmanna Sögur*, *Þáttr Egils Hallssonar ok Tófa Valgautssonar*, Valgautr tells his wife that if he is slain, then she should hold an erfiöl. Afterwards she should build a pyre, place his body and all the wealth she can upon the pyre, and then throw herself into the flames. This seems somewhat reminiscent of the Anglo-Saxon archbishop Ælfric's implication that funeral feasts took place before the disposal of the body. Of course, it must be consider that *Þáttr Egils Hallssonar ok Tófa Valgautssonar* is a very late, even a very romanticised account and may not be particularly accurate in many of its details.

Þáttr Egils Hallssonar ok Tófa Valgautssonar also differs from both *Laxdæla Saga* and *Gísla Saga* in that Valgautr expresses the desire to be burned in a pyre, while *Laxdæla Saga* and *Gísla Saga* the bodies are disposed of through burial. Cremation does appear elsewhere in Old Norse and Icelandic literature and is mentioned in Arabic traveller Ibn Fadlan's account of the Rus. Perhaps the most famous portrayal of a cremation is the tale of the funeral of Baldr told in the *Prose Edda*. There Snorri states that the gods took Baldr's body to the sea, where his ship Hringhorni awaited on the shore. The gods could not budge the ship to set it to sea; even four berserks could not move it. The ettinwife Hyrrokkin finally pushed the ship out to sea, so hard that fire burst from the rollers. The body of Barldr was then placed on the ship, whereupon his wife Nanna died from grief at the sight. She was placed upon the ship with him. The pyre was then lit. Þórr hallowed the pyre with Mjölnir. Óðinn place the ring Draupnir upon the pyre and Baldr's horse went upon it as well.

Ibn Fadlan described the funeral of a chieftain among the Rus that took place on the Volga (what would be modern day Bulgaria) in the tenth century. Ibn Fadlan stated that they placed the chieftain in a temporary grave and made clothes for him. His family asked his slaves who among them would die with him and a slave girl volunteered. From that point forward she was accompanied everywhere and her every need was seen to. She drank and sang every day.

On the day of the funeral, a ship was drawn up on the shore and placed on a wooden structure. They made a pavilion on board the ship into which an old woman, whom Ibn Fadlan calls the "Angel of Death," places various furnishings. The corpse was then removed from the temporary grave and dressed in trousers, stockings, boots, tunics, a caftan, and a hat. They placed the corpse on the ship and placed various fruits, bread, meat, and onions with him. They killed a dog and placed it on the ship. They also placed the dead man's weapons by his side. Two horses were slain and placed on the ship. They then killed a rooster and a hen and threw them on the ship.

The slave girl then went to each tent and had sex with the owner of the tent. She told each of them that she did this out of love for her master. Later she was lead to a structure resembling a door frame. They raised her and she said that she saw her father and her mother. They raised her a second time and she said that she saw all of her dead kinsmen. They raised her a third time and she said she saw her master in paradise. She was then taken aboard the ship where she sang and then drank an intoxicating drink. She was then forced into the pavilion where six men had intercourse with her. She was then placed beside her master and the Angel of Death killed her.

The dead man's kinsmen then lit the ship on fire. Where the ship had burned they erected a monument.

It is difficult to gauge the accuracy of Ibn Fadlan's account. It must be kept in mind that he did not know Old Norse and had to work through an interpreter. It must also be kept in mind that eyewitness accounts are not always reliable. It could be significant that Ibn Faldlan's account features events that are not mentioned in accounts of other funerals. For example, Ibn Fadlan tells us first that the girl had sex with each owner of each tent and then had sex with six men who entered the pavilion. In other accounts of funerals, sex is never mentioned as taking place. Indeed, it must be questioned how Ibn Fadlan even knew what went on within the tents or the pavilion. It is possible that he simply misunderstood his interpreter or simply assumed that sex was taking place. Similarly, there is no figure quite like the Angel of Death appearing in the whole of Germanic literature.

Regardless, some of the features found in Ibn Fadlan's account are found in the account of other Scandinavian funerals from the Viking Age. Among these is the preparation of the body before it is cremated or buried. Old Norse and Icelandic literature has only a little to say as to what treatment a dead body received prior to cremation or burial. It does seem that immediately after death the *nábjargir* (literally "corpse help") had to be performed. This was the closing of the eyes, mouth,

68

and nostrils of the dead. In *Eyrbyggja Saga*, when the wicked Þórolf Clubfoot died, Arnkell warned no one to step into the house until the nábjargir was performed. Apparently this was for fear that Þórolf's corpse might give people the evil eye The nábjargir is also mentioned in *Egils Saga* as having been performed on Skallagrim's corpse following his death. Beyond the nábjargir, corpses were prepared burial or cremation in other ways. In *Gísla Saga* it is told how men must be outfitted with *helskór* (literally "Hel Shoes"), so that they might be able to walk to the "Other World".

Another feature Ibn Fadlan's account shares with Old Norse and Icelandic accounts is the placement of goods and animals upon the pyre. Both evidence from Old Norse and Icelandic literature confirm that this portion of Ibn Fadlan's account is probably true. In *Ynglinga Saga* among the laws that Óðinn established was that all dead men should be burned and their belongings placed on the pyre. This is reflected in Baldr's funeral from the *Prose Edda*, in which his body is burned alongside the ring Draupnir and his horse. Of course, it must be pointed out that Ibn Fadlan's account, Óðinn's decree from the *Ynglinga Saga*, and the account of Baldr's funeral from the *Prose Edda* are all three reminiscent of Beowulf's funeral. Of course, goods and animals were not only burned alongside the dead, but often buried with the dead in mounds. *Egils Saga* tells how Skallagrim's weapons, his horse, and his smithing tools were placed in the mound with him. *Laxdæla Saga* makes reference to treasure being buried with Unn and some goods, though not many, being buried with Höskuldr.

Another feature that Ibn Fadlan's account shares with other accounts of Scandinavian funerals from the Viking Age is that the dead were burned in a ship. In the *Prose Edda* Baldr is also burned in a ship. Not only were ships burned on pyres, but ships were also buried in mounds, much like the ship burial at

Sutton Hoo in England. In *Gísla Saga* it is told how a boulder was placed on a ship within a mound, presumably so it would not move. *Laxdæla Saga* tells how Unn's body was laid in a ship within her mound.

There is plenty of archaeological evidence for both ship burials and good being placed within graves. With regards to ships, many ship burials have been found in Scandinavia, some dating to as early as the sixth century. Ship burials have also been discovered in areas settled by the Vikings, such as the Isle of Man.[7] A grave at Oseberg in Norway contained a ship about 68 feet in length, which contained the bodies of two women. The grave at Oseberg also held a number of grave goods. There were several carved, wooden items, as well as an exquisite processional waggon.[8] That animals were also killed and placed in the grave or on the pyre, as in Ibn Fadlan's account, is also borne out by archaeological evidence. The Oseberg grave also contains the bodies of at least thirteen horses.[9]

As mentioned earlier, among the Scandinavians and Icelanders, the erfiöl appears to have taken place after the burial or cremation for the most part. In Saxo's *Gesta Danorum*, the hero Starkað states that the funeral of a king must include a drinking bout. And this is indeed the form that the erfiöl appears to take in Old Norse and Icelandic sources. In *Ynglinga Saga* in *Heimskringla*, Snorri states that it was the custom that the host of an erfiöl should sit upon the footstool before the high seat until the *bragarfull* had been made. He would then drink the bragarfull and take serous vows that must be fulfilled afterwards. He would then take his place upon the high seat.

Also in *Heimskinga*, an erfiöl is described in *Ólafs Saga Tryggvasonar* in even more detail. Upon the death of Harald, his son Sveinn arranged for his erfiöl. At the erfiöl he sat upon the high seat and drank a *minni* to his father. He then vowed that before three winters had passed, he would either kill King Æþelræd of England or drive him from the country. Everyone then drank. The chief of the Jomsborg Vikings then drank a horn. Everyone at the feast then drank a minni to Jesus. After that a minni was drank to St. Michael. Jarl Sigvaldi then drank a minii to his father and vowed the before three winters had passed he would go to Norway and kill Jarl Hákon or drive him from the country. His brother Þorkell then made a vow to follow him to Norway and never flinch from the battle so long as Sigvaldi remained. Bue the Thick then followed to follow them all to Norway and to leave until he had killed Þorkel Leira and bedded his daughter Ingibjörg.

Among the Scandinavians and Icelanders, the erfiöl was more than just a feast held in honour of someone who had recently died. It was also the time when the dead man's heirs claimed their inheritance. This is demonstrated in both *Ynglinga Saga* and *Ólafs Saga Tryggvasonar*. In *Ynglinga Saga* the heir must sit on the footstool before the high seat and can only claim his place upon the high seat after drinking the bragarfull. In *Ólafs Saga Tryggvasonar* Svein takes his place upon the high seat and then drinks a minni to his father. It must be noted that Snorri contradicts himself in stating that an heir cannot take the high seat until the bragarfull is drank. but then portraying Svein as already seated in the high seat when he makes his minni. Perhaps this of little importance; it is the fact that this is the point at which an heir claims his inheritance that is significant.

Beyond being the time when heirs claim their inheritance, it would seem that the erfiöl is the drinking bout of which Starkað spoke in *Gesta Danorum*. This is particularly true of *Ólafs Saga Tryggvasonar*. In the erfiöl portrayed there, individuals drink and take oaths in turn. This is extremely reminiscent of the rite of symbel, in which individuals drink and utter important words in turn. In fact, the only difference

71

between the two would appear to be that an erfiöl is held in honour of the recently dead and includes the claiming of inheritance by the dead man's heirs, while symbel does not.

Ynglinga Saga indicates that the erfiöl's first toast was the bragrafull, while *Ólafs Saga Tryggvasonar* indicates that the first toast was a minni to the dead King Harald. It seems that to some small degree that the words *bragarfull* and *minni* must have been interchangeable. The word *bragarfull* appears to literally mean "cup of the foremost" or "cup of the chief". It appears primarily in the context of funeral feasts, although it also appears in the context of blóts. In *Hákonar Saga goða* Snorri states that following toasts to Óðinn, Njörðr, and Freyr, the bragarfull was drank. The word *minni* means "memory", "memorial", and hence "memorial cup". It seems possible that the bragarfull was the cup drank to the memory of a dead chieftain or dead chieftains. As such, it would automatically be a *minni*--a memorial cup.

According to *Ólafs Saga Tryggvasonar*, once Svein made the minni to the late King Harald, everyone drank. It would appear that everyone present was expected to drink to the memory of the dead man. The leader of the Jomsborg Vikings then drank a horn. Unfortunately, Snorri does not tell us the nature of his toast, so that we have no way of knowing what was said at this point in the erfiöl. Following that toast, a minni was drank to Jesus and then a minni to St. Michael. Naturally, toasts to Jesus and St. Michael probably would not have taken place among heathen, although it seems like that at this point in an erfiöl the ancient heathen Scandinavians may have made toasts to the gods. Once they had converted to Christianity, Jesus and St. Michael would have been substituted for the gods.

Following these toasts, it appears that the efiöl in *Ólafs Saga Tryggvasonar* proceeded much as a symbel. In turn, various individuals take oaths to accomplish various deeds (all of which seem to include going to Norway to kill Jarl Hákon…).

In his condemnation of funeral feasts among the Anglo-Saxons, Ælfric made reference to "heathen songs" sang at these rituals. Neither *Ynglinga Saga* nor *Ólafs Saga Tryggvasonar* make reference to any such songs. According to *Landnámabók*, however, at an erfiöl Odd performed a death song he had composed in memory of Hjalti.

From Old Norse and Icelandic sources, it would appear that upon death the nábjargir was performed. The body would then be cremated or buried. Afterwards, perhaps immediately or perhaps several months later, the erfiöl would be held. The erfiöl would proceed in a manner similar to a symbel. It would open with a minni to the recently deceased, following which the heirs would claim their inheritance. Afterwars boasts to the gods may have been drank, followed by boasts of the sort seen in symbel, in which individuals take oaths to perform various deeds.

Funerals Among Modern Heathen

Using the funerals portrayed in Old English, Old Norse, and Icelandic sources, it is possible to construct a funeral ceremony for use among modern heathen with some degree of authenticity. It could perhaps proceed as follows:

1. Burial or Cremation: From the funerals in *Béowulf*, it seems apparent that some sort of ritual took place during cremation among the ancient Germanic peoples. During the cremation of Hnæf's body it is said that a woman lamented with songs. During the cremation of Beowulf his widow sounded his passing. While the singing of death songs is not portrayed at burials, it seems quite likely that they did take place. Beyond the singing of a death song, another rite that

73

might have taken place at cremations was the hallowing of the balefire. In the *Prose Edda* it is said how Þórr hallowed Baldr's pyre with his hammer. Although this is never said to take place at burials, it may well have. Indeed, this may well be indicated by the large number of memorial stones in Scandinavia dating from the Viking Age that read *Þur viki* "May Þórr hallow…" If runes were inscribed asking Þórr to hallow the stone and perhaps the mound as well, it seems likely that words were uttered to that effect upon the interment of the dead.

Of course, today open cremation is illegal in the United States. Fortunately, most crematoriums permit family and friends to be present during cremation and even to perform those religious rituals the family believes necessary. In the case of burial, graveside services are universally accepted. At either a cremation or burial, then, a death song should perhaps be sung and hallowing should take place.

From the funerals in *Béowulf* and those portrayed in Old Norse and Icelandic sources, not to mention from archaeological evidence we know that goods were either buried or burned with the dead. Short of erecting a mausoleum, it is probably not possible to bury a body with the extravagant goods (swords, shields, helmets, treasure, and so on) that he ancient heathen interred with the dead. It is impossible to do so in the case of modern cremation. This does not mean that modern heathen must abandon this custom. The dead can be buried or burned with jewellery and other precious belongings, as well as money to represent the wealth with which the dead in ancient times were buried.

2. Erfiöl or the Funeral "Feast": From Old Norse and Icelandic sources, the erfiöl appears to have been a well-established custom. There is less evidence for funeral "feasts" among the Anglo-Saxons, though it seems likely that they also practised this custom. From Old Norse and Icelandic sources it seems apparent that the erfiöl resembled a symbel to a large degree. It could proceed as follows:

A: The Minni: The primary heirs drink the minni to the dead. Once the primary heirs have drank the minni to the dead, everyone present should also drink to the dead's memory.

B. The Claiming of the Inheritance: The primary heirs claim their inheritance. This could be represented by sitting in a symbolic "high seat" or place of honour.

C. The Gods Are Honoured: Boasts are then made to the gods.

D. Oaths: Oaths are then made by those who wish to make them. These would probably resemble the gielps and béots of symbel. Alternatively, those who wish to drink another minni or sing a death song may do so.

Endnotes

1. Ellis Davidson, H. R. *The Lost Beliefs of Northern Europe*, p. 134.
2. Ellis Davidson, H. R. *The Lost Beliefs of Northern Europe*, pp. 18-19
3. *ibid.*
4. *ibid.*
5 Bauschatz, Paul C. *The Well and the Tree*, pp. 55-57.
6. Lang, Andrew. Curiosities of Parish Registers", http://www.bookrags.com/books/bkbkm/PART4.htm
7. Ellis David, H. R. Ellis. *The Lost Beliefs of Northern Europe*. p. 19
8. *ibid.*
9. *ibid.*

Wordhoard

Bragarfull: The "boast of the foremost", the boast that may have been made to dead chieftains.

Erfiöl: The Old Norse "feast" or drinking bout at which the recently dead were honoured and the heirs claimed their inheritance. In modern terms, quite simply, a funeral.

Minii: A cup drank in memory of the dead.

Nábjargir: The last services of the dead, in which the eyes, nostrils, and mouth are closed.

Bookhoard

Cleasby, Richard. Vigfusson, Gudbrand (eds.). *An Icelandic-English Dictionary*. Oxford: Clarendon Press. 1975

Ellis Davidson, H.R. *The Lost Beliefs of Northern Europe*. London: Routledge 1993

Hall, Clark (ed.) *A Concise Anglo-Saxon Dictionary*. Downsview, Canada: University of Toronto Press.

Turville-Petere, E.O.G. *Myth and Religion of the North*. New York: Holt, Rineheart, and Winston. 1964

Wodening, Eric. "An Anglo-Saxon Symbel", pp. 11-20. *Theod*, Waelburges, 1995.

Abbreviations

CE: Common Era, indicating years dated from the foundation of the Roman Empire.

OE: Old English. English spoken prior to 1100 CE

ON: Old Norse, the Norse language spoken prior to 1300 CE.

Printed in Great Britain
by Amazon

52490360R00047